IS THIS
SEAT
FOR ME?

IS THIS SEAT FOR ME?

OVERCOMING IMPOSTER SYNDROME

in Everyday Life and Business

SHEILA M. BUSWELL

with contributions by
Stacey Brown. Sheila Buswell. Mary Imani. Kate Mansker.

Printed in the United States of America.
First paperback edition May 2023.

Cover and layout design by G Sharp Design, LLC.
www.gsharpmajor.com

ISBN: 978-1-959555-66-7 (paperback)

ACKNOWLEDGMENTS

This book contains contributions from people in my life I admire. What follows are the real-life stories of real people who have struggled with insecurity and self-doubt and have discovered ways to overcome these feelings. But it remains an ongoing struggle, and every day each of us works hard to get through it. I think of how their stories could help young people navigate life and find their seat at the table. After all, no one should have to let the circumstances they are subjected to define them. Everyone should be given the chance to thrive.

I would be grateful to sit at a table with any of the people who contributed to this book. Ingrid, Mary, Kate, Peter, Roz, Stacey, and Betsey are all superstars, and I want to thank them for their friendship, and for offering to tell their stories so I can share them with you.

I hope the things we have all learned will help you find your own seat at the table.

I definitely want to thank my parents and family for instilling in me a sense that I have value. Your love has carried me through some very difficult circumstances.

I wish I had thanked and asked my sister Brigid more—she is in my thoughts a lot.

I also want to thank my husband, Gregg, who loves me at my worst. For him, I aspire to be my best.

TABLE OF CONTENTS

Acknowledgments v

Preface xi
Imposter Syndrome

Chapter 1   A Story of Business and Babies 1
Nontraditional Imposter Syndrome

Chapter 2   Thank You for Your Service 25
By Stacey Brown

Chapter 3   Playing Varsity. 33

Chapter 4   Ingrid the Imposter 41
A Career Path like Chutes and Ladders

Chapter 5   Am I Really a Duck? 51
The Danger of Imposter Syndrome During a Career Change

Chapter 6   Overachieving/Overworking 57
An Imposter Syndrome Journey

Chapter 7   Not Letting What is Done to Me Define Me. 63
Recovering from Imposter Syndrome

Chapter 8   A Seat at the Table 69
I Belong Here

Chapter 9   A Place at the Table 75
Now Seating Imposter Syndrome, Party of ... You?

Part 1   Cultural Solutions 81

Part 2   Personal Solutions 89

Notes on Contributors 105

"If there's a book that you want
to read, but it hasn't been written
yet, then you must write it."

—*Toni Morrison*

"Data are just summaries of thousands of stories—tell a few of those stories to help make the data meaningful."

—*Dan Heath*

PREFACE

IMPOSTER SYNDROME

By Sheila Buswell

I hate being bad at things. And I've always felt like I was bad at the things I was "supposed" to be good at. Being around groups of women and babies is one example. In these situations, I spend much of my time mentally pleading, "Please don't put your baby in my lap." It isn't that I don't like babies—I just don't enjoy the experience of holding them. I also don't feel like I belong in groups of women in general. I instantly become insecure. I hate this feeling, so until recently I avoided those groups whenever possible.

Often, when I step out of my comfort zone, I start doubting myself. This isn't an uncommon experience for many people, but I never put a name to it. I simply endured or avoided situations that made me feel this way. But life soon showed me that running away wasn't always an option—especially if I wanted to pursue my goals. Luckily, I never had to deal professionally with groups of women or babies, so that particular fear never got in my way. But there were many others ready to take its place.

I previously had a career where I never questioned myself or my position professionally; I never really had to step outside my comfort zone. But all that changed when I left my full-time job on August 6,

2019. I had invented a medical mobility device controlled by Artificial Intelligence. I had to learn a great deal about business and computer engineering to create my new business, Buswell Biomedical.

I learned a lot in my first year. Some lessons were enlightening, others were extremely harsh. One of the harshest was that engineering was not the most critical thing in a business; the product I invented was not the most important part of my work. This was a difficult thing to hear. Product development is significant, but business foundations and structures, in many ways, matter more. I was learning a new technology and a new field, and the most important thing I learned was that I needed to keep learning.

It has been several years since I started my business, and I have grown a great deal. I gained knowledge about both computer engineering and business, but I am not yet completely comfortable with either subject. Other people noticed my discomfort as I moved into this new phase of my life, and they labeled it as "imposter syndrome."

The people who labeled this as imposter syndrome weren't ill-intentioned, but their comments did not sit well with me. After some self-reflection, I realized I do indeed have imposter syndrome, but not in the areas they thought. I'm in my element when it comes to discussing materials, programming, price structure, and sensors. On the other hand, talking about makeup, hair, and diapers, I feel like an imposter. Gender stereotypes may lead one to assume it should be the other way around—after all, women are "supposed" to be good with babies and bad at business. But my personal experience didn't match that.

Imposter syndrome is a psychological phenomenon where individuals doubt their accomplishments and have a persistent fear of being exposed as a fraud, even when there is evidence to suggest otherwise. Simply stated, it is a feeling of not being "enough." People experiencing imposter syndrome can feel like they don't deserve to be where they are, and they worry that they will be discovered as incompetent or fraudulent.

Often associated with high-achieving individuals, imposter syndrome can affect people from all walks of life, regardless of their age, gender, or profession. While it is difficult to estimate the exact number of people who are affected by imposter syndrome, studies have shown that an estimated 70% of people experience it at some point in their lives. In many cases, imposter syndrome is believed to hinder professional performance and lead to burnout, but it is worth noting that it can manifest differently in different people. The severity and frequency of symptoms also varies. Some people may experience its symptoms only occasionally, while others may struggle with them constantly. Overall, imposter syndrome is a common experience, and it is important to remember that it is often a normal response to challenging situations.

In spite of how commonly it occurs, imposter syndrome is not an accepted psychological disorder. The term was first used in 1966. There is an often-cited study that was completed in 1978, entitled "The imposter phenomenon in high achieving women: Dynamics and Therapeutic intervention." This, along with further studies, may show how imposter syndrome impacts women and minorities to a more significant degree. Perhaps not coincidentally, many of the contributors to this book are women and/or people of color.

Here's the thing: I do believe in imposter syndrome. As a book who was continuously judged by its cover, I've experienced it firsthand. For me, it seems that this is always where it starts: with the fact that too often, people judge others based solely on their appearance. In my case, for instance, people expect me to be good at holding babies and bad at math and engineering—of course, the opposite is true. Similarly, the minorities in the world and the women in my field will never "look" like the people who traditionally held those roles. Nevertheless, they are often told they need to look and act a certain way to access certain spaces or positions. So, once they achieve placement in those positions and spaces, it makes sense that they would feel like imposters. No one has ever told them they belong or even allowed them to act naturally. With those internalized messages, it is incredibly difficult not to feel like a fraud.

As I put together this book, I reached out to many wonderful people in my life who had also experienced insecurity and doubt. I asked them to contribute their stories to reveal what these feelings look like in different contexts and different lives. Together, through sharing their experiences, and my own, we will explore this all-too-common feeling of "not being good enough." The feeling that you don't quite fit in is a natural one, as is the self-doubt that often comes with it—but these can be overcome. I call this quest for self-confidence and self-assuredness, *Is This Seat For Me?* Everyone deserves to sit at a table where they belong—a table where they can learn something but not feel as though they are out of their depth. A place they can contribute and have their contributions valued. This book is one such place.

I feel like part of the reason that the focus of imposter syndrome is often on women and minorities is because they are the only ones brave enough to talk about it. (Of the numerous men whom I asked to contribute to this book, only one actually did.) But my suspicion is that, as humans, we all have these feelings of self-doubt to a certain extent, and that is why I wanted to write this book: to start an open, honest, and courageous dialog in which people can share their various experiences of imposter syndrome, as well as their various solutions to it. No matter who we are, or how it manifests for us, I believe that this is how we can get through it: together.

Please use this book as a kind of guide. I hope it will give you some wonderful role models, as well as some practical solutions to overcome the various ways imposter syndrome can affect us. I hope the stories of the real people in this book will inspire you to move past the obstacles in your own life so that you can become an even better version of yourself.

I put my energy into making myself feel as though I belong at all the tables where I sit. Still, I struggle every day, and so do the other contributors. I am not an expert, nor are any of us; we are all works in progress. But when we sit at the right table with the right people, we can accomplish great things.

CHAPTER ONE

A STORY OF BUSINESS AND BABIES

NONTRADITIONAL IMPOSTER SYNDROME

By Sheila Buswell

"If life were predictable it would cease
to be life and would be without flavor."

—*Eleanor Roosevelt*

The Early Years

I grew up the youngest of eight children. As a child, I was not motivated by the same things as my siblings. I was potty-trained by age one, could read at the age of three, and my siblings were sick of my attitude by age five. I was a spoiled brat and was accustomed to getting what I wanted. I never had low self-esteem; in fact, I may have had the opposite problem. Everyone thought I was great, and so did I; I was never told differently.

Intelligence was the most valuable trait in my family. I remember one day my sister was voted "Most Beautiful" at the high school in our hometown. When she came home bragging about it, the topic shifted quickly to her academics. Her grades, SAT Score, ACT Score. The schools she got into. For my family, it was more important to value intelligence, which they believed was a more permanent and useful quality than beauty.

This worked out well for me because I was smart. I never spent time learning about makeup and hair, as I didn't value those pursuits, and I was often bugged by how much time my sisters spent on them. While this fit with my family's ideals, it also left me feeling like not enough around other women for much of my life. I marveled at how well they did hair and makeup, but I just didn't think this was a skill I would need. I never babysat, either. (Diapers are just gross and babies even then seemed fragile.) In the end, even though not learning about those things was my choice, those situations made me feel insecure, and sometimes still do. I am in my forties now and have generally found that my parents' views were right. My intelligence has stayed with me; in fact, I might even say I am smarter now. I know my worth, even if I can't do my makeup.

I was accused of being stuck up in high school. I thought I was smart and funny, and I felt it wasn't my problem if someone else wasn't either of those things. I was insecure and mean—not a happy combination. I am now secure, but at the time I had a lot of growing to do.

Even though I was smart, I didn't get good grades. (My siblings, on the other hand, did.) I was not motivated to learn things I thought were pointless. I was motivated to learn things I thought I would use later. If I didn't think it was worth learning, I didn't bother retaining it.

I got great grades in the third grade, and I tested well. But I didn't like the "gifted and talented" class teacher, so I almost failed 4th grade. I actively did poorly on purpose. Later, I was removed from history class, as I didn't see the point. I exhibited this character flaw as a ten-year-old; I'm 46 now, and I still react like this at work. Historically, when I do not like my boss or workplace, I do not perform.

Defiance has always been part of my brand. As a child, if I was told I couldn't do something, that was exactly what I would do. Unsurprisingly, I received many disciplinary notes home. The books I was eager to read were "banned," which was exactly why I wanted to read them, whether they were good or not. Also, I wasn't allowed to watch TV unless I got straight A's—so almost all the TV I watched required me to break the rules to do so.

My rebellion against authority was sometimes positive, though. Later, I ran two marathons. I am certain it was due to a doctor telling me I would not be able to run again. My desire to prove people wrong has followed me my whole life, through the good and the bad. When I worked hard to learn something, it was generally due to being told there was a reason "I couldn't." My will to prove "them" wrong overcame whatever imposter syndrome theme played in my head. It has been said I am an overachiever, but I think I just don't want to be told I can't do things.

This defiance of convention wasn't just part of my childhood; it spread into my adulthood and was a big contributor to my confidence. People expected that I would look and behave a certain way just because I was a woman. But I pride myself on not looking like anything that is on my resume.

Scholarship Loss

I didn't work all that hard to get through high school. But I still graduated third in my class and received a scholarship to the University of Utah. Growing up, I had thick glasses and braces, and I thought looking smart was enough to make me smart. College changed my perspective on this. One provision of that scholarship was that I had to maintain a 3.8 GPA, and I did not. I may have looked smart—and the truth is I *was* smart—but I didn't work. As Tim Notke put it, "Hard work beats talent when talent doesn't work hard." Before my first year was up, I had lost my scholarship.

I made up for not working my first year by overworking my second year. But in spite of my shift in work-ethic, I simply wasn't set up well for success. I worked full time to pay for my education at ARUP Inc. processing specimens at night. I went to class during the day and slept when I could. I did not sleep nearly enough, and this did not help my grades; they further declined. I was thin, and my eyes were sunken. I fell asleep anywhere I managed to sit still for a moment. I went to class one day, sat in the front middle seat to stay awake, and fell asleep. The Professor was leaving when I woke up—I'd missed the entire lecture.

I went for a long run to do some thinking. I knew that something had to change. After some serious soul-searching, I decided to leave school temporarily and join the Army. I had to get a waiver for my eyesight, which meant my options for a Military Occupational Specialty (MOS) were limited. I had a high Armed Services Vocational Aptitude Battery Test (ASVAB) and General Technical (GT) score. I ended up a 63J (Quartermaster and Chemical Equipment Repairer).

Military Time

I cross-trained as a Generator Mechanic (52D). I became good at fixing generators to avoid detail (aka cleaning toilets). I was attached to a Tanker Battalion 1-35, and I was Shop Foreman by the time my service ended.

The Army was the first workplace where I experienced a true meritocracy. During my time there, people quickly learned to distinguish between the soldier who looked like they could fix your generator and the person who could actually fix it. In the field, this was picked up fast. If you wanted your lights on, it mattered more that the soldier was able to get your generator to put out power, not how competent they appeared.

My best friend in the army exemplified all this. She didn't LOOK like a generator mechanic—she was beautiful and feminine—but she was great at what she did. She was a competent soldier, and a valued friend and colleague. She was driven and smart, and the only one I know from my time in the military who finished their schooling. She used the military not as a career but as a stepping stone into a better life for herself and her family.

Having the support of someone who was so intelligent and driven, while also being kind and feminine, was invaluable to me. I often wonder, if my best friend and I didn't have each other, what would have happened? I was so lucky to cross paths with a like-minded soul at that time in my life. We traveled when we had money or played

"Jacks" in the hallway of the barracks when we didn't. We laughed at the drunk "Barracks Rats," who never left the base no matter what. She was the only girlfriend I had that I really did girlfriend stuff with. I would kill or die for her, but we soaked our feet and wore silly masks instead. I haven't had many friends in my life, and having her made a huge impact on me. I am in my mid-forties now and I can say that for whatever reason this was the only time in my life I felt comfortable and not like an imposter doing "girly stuff."

If she knocked on my door today and asked me to help her hide a body, I wouldn't ask questions—I would go get a shovel. I don't need bullets taken for me. What I need, and what we've always had, is real allegiance.

Transitioning

Getting out of the military was not easy; we were often told we would be back in the Army or flipping burgers within six months. When I got out, California was in the middle of an energy crisis, and I was lucky enough to be faced with two good choices. I could make good money as a Generator Technician, or I could go back to school. I ended up in Missouri at University of Missouri-Rolla, now Missouri University of Science and Technology.

When I went back to school, I didn't know the difference between a derivative and an integral. To get to the point where I did know, I busted my ass. I was often in the math help center from when it opened until it closed. My journey through mathematics showed me the harm that can happen when people judge someone based on assumptions. For instance, some people expect that just because I am a woman, I'm not good at math. Other people say things like, "You're an engineer—of course you're good at math!"

The implication is that I didn't work—that math comes to me easily. But the truth is it took effort and struggle, and if it was a gift, it was a gift I earned with sweat and tears, not one that was just given to me. I applied myself and worked hard to relearn math concepts—it is very upsetting when people make assumptions that undermine my efforts.

Gendered Expectations

I moved from school into engineering. I had spent such a long time being so driven and working so hard that I came into the industry with very little self-doubt. When my assigned mentor suggested that I was not going to be taken seriously as an engineer unless I stopped acting "so girly," I thought this was insane. I'd been in the Army as a generator mechanic (not exactly girly work). I'd earned an engineering degree with great grades and high test scores. Her concerns revealed more about her reality than they did about mine. After all, this woman knew nothing about me; she was assigned as my mentor because she was female, nothing more.

Looking back, I realize she was revealing the reality of the place we worked. It was sad, but it was true. Many women engineers did what they thought they needed to do to be taken seriously. When I finished my bachelor's degree in Mechanical Engineering in 2005, women only comprised 18% of college graduates in mechanical engineering nationwide at that time, and it was significantly lower in the Midwest. In 2020, that number had only grown to 20%—a slow improvement, to be sure (these statistics are from the National Center for Education Statistics). From my perspective, the number of women engineers shrank as my career progressed. I was often the only woman in a big room. I rarely had female co-workers and never had a female boss. Even though I was among fellow professionals, my gender left me isolated and lacking support.

At my first job, I was not only assigned a mentor, but I also had three mentees of my own. One came to me in tears when her boss mentioned in her review that she wore her hair in a ponytail every day. When I asked her boss to point out a time when he referred to a man's hair in his review, he not only yelled at me, but he also told my boss. I was unimpressed; yelling at someone who has spent time in the military is silly. No one can yell as well as a Drill Sergeant.

I was sent to California for three months because of my inquiry. I left that job soon after. If you think that was a long time ago and this sort of thing doesn't happen anymore, you're wrong. It was 2007—nowhere near long enough ago to excuse that kind of behavior.

I stayed at my first job out of college for two years before leaving the extremely sexist workplace for what I thought would be greener pastures at a new company. Unfortunately, future jobs only got more sexist, a trend that continued for my next five jobs. I have stories that felt to me that they belong in the 1970s. It was hard to think that there was so little progression over so many years and so many locations.

At my next engineering job, I was often sent pictures of Sarah Palin in a bikini. These photos were poorly photoshopped, even for 2007. I was harassed and experienced daily microaggressions I was once emailed a tattooed vagina. When I complained to Human Resources, the guy that I complained about was sent to "sensitivity training." During this training, he continued to behave poorly. He would sit in a 23-year-old woman's cubicle and just wait for her, while she hid in my cube praying for him to leave. I was furious at the company for allowing this type of behavior. It was explained to me once that this engineer had many patents and was very valuable.

Apparently, this kind of toxic behavior was tolerated when it was directed towards people who were not as "valuable" as the perpetrator.

Later, I was laid off from this job at the same time as this guy. I was told that to keep my severance pay, I was not allowed to leverage any lawsuit. I learned this was not uncommon. I don't know if it is lawful, but I know it is wrong.

Even as a woman in a male-saturated industry, I never doubted that I belonged at the table. But I count myself lucky for this. It would have been easy in this sort of outdated, misogynistic environment to begin to doubt myself and fall prey to imposter syndrome. Understandably, many in my position would feel out of place, and in trying to fit in, would end up feeling like they didn't belong. Me, I had proved myself in the Army and in school, and I was determined to prove myself here, too, regardless of how I was perceived. No, I never felt like I didn't belong at the table; but I did feel that these awful people did not deserve to sit at the table with me. I hated that company for their terrible reaction to my complaint, and after that, I found great difficulty being motivated to work at all for them. This doesn't mean there weren't good men at the company; I actually met my husband there. But even though positive role models are actually in the majority, they get overshadowed by the people who exhibit this toxic behavior. How can innovation occur if this kind of workplace environment is tolerated? Not only does it affect the people involved, but it also affects anyone that witnesses it, which can be demoralizing. If society wants the benefits of a diverse workplace, there needs to be a push to root out toxic behavior like this and stop rewarding it. Skill should never be valued over character.

At my next full-time job, I was the only female engineer, and, perhaps not coincidentally, the only engineer without an office. I was routinely put in inferior working conditions. The company claimed they supported veterans, but other engineers with less time and no veteran status had better situations. Eventually we were all downgraded. I was also downgraded—not to a cube, as that would have been an upgrade from where I was—but from my current hallway to a smaller hallway.

I was fired from that job after two years; my replacement lasted a week. I did not view this female engineer as my competition, but I knew as soon as they interviewed another woman that I was going to lose my job.

There is a Friedrich Nietzsche quote—"He who has a why to live for can bear almost any how." My why was: I wanted to learn more about biomedical engineering. This was my passion, and I was not going to let bad experiences keep me out of a field that I loved and valued. I invested in getting a master's degree. I wanted to fight assumptions with education.

St. Louis, where I currently live and have always worked as an engineer, was recently ranked as one of the worst cities for women in technical fields. In another study, it was noted that the tech field here lacked diversity. This has been my reality. I have been here since I graduated in 2005. I have older sisters living in the Bay Area, and they too have STEM (Science, Technology, Engineering, Math) degrees. I do not think they have stories like this, but I don't know for certain—I am no longer close enough to them to ask. There has been a drive to increase diversity in STEM careers. Yet every office of engineers I have worked in had the same demographic. I think the culture needs to change to allow for a different demographic. I know my field of mechanical engineering and biomedical engineering exceedingly well. I took all the classes to ensure I knew what I was talking about. I made certain I came from a place of authority. I could handle any question if I applied my education. And when I was questioned, I would refer to my degrees and publications to prove I could build a case. I worked hard to know my stuff. I had to work harder than most of the people around me, even though I was just as good or better than them. I feel as though many of them "looked the part" and so were permitted to do the minimum. If you don't "look" a certain way, you tend to do more to make up for it—and often feel like an imposter anyway.

I don't know how common this mindset is; in truth I have rarely had female coworkers, much less a female boss. And the women I have worked with have been very competitive. They know there is very little room in the field, so they behave as if they must take out the competition. As a result, we never really got to bond over our shared situations. This, to me, is something else that desperately needs to change. Empowered people empower other people. By contrast, some of the women I worked with were the first to create obstacles. They would use information I'd expressed to them in confidence as ammunition against me. I do not view women as my competition. I am an engineer; I just want to solve problems. I want to produce the best product, plain and simple, and if an idea is great, that is what should matter—not the gender of the person who came up with it.

My last full-time job as an engineer was in 2019. I was continually asked to "smile more" and was challenged about materials in meetings. My MS is very materials-intensive, so to say I know my stuff would not be an understatement. In a meeting, I was interrupted and told titanium is stronger than steel. Basically, steel is stronger by any traditional metric, but for anyone reading this who doesn't know, it is not that simple. There are alloys of steel that are weak, and alloys of titanium that are strong. This same person that challenged me inquired if I felt OK working in a male-dominated field. This seemed a strange question to me, as I had been in this field for fifteen years. I also came from the Army, which even today is not known for having a large female presence. This behavior was intended to intimidate, but it was not overt. I was prepared for it, and I was armed with knowledge in my field, and had no doubt about my seat at that table. However, I had severe doubts about his seat at that table with me.

As part of my job, I tested materials and wrote test plans. I worked very frequently with engineers in other departments. If those other engineers don't respect you, it is difficult, if not impossible, to get anything done. In 2019, I was 42, and I was told by a person with a BS in Mechanical Engineering in a different department who had less education than me that I would "be HOT if I grew my hair out and dyed it…" If he talked to me this way, how would he speak to the 22-year-old woman that recently graduated with a BS? When would this stop?

I expected the challenge in the meeting, and I was prepared for it. I was not prepared for my "hotness" to be assessed by this individual. I guess my question is simply: Is this something that must be dealt with forever? Would I always be judged not as an expert in materials, but as an object? This attitude should have changed 30 years ago!

And if I was viewed as an object, how would a young woman, attractive or not, be treated? Is that the best the new engineering grad can hope for? Why did she bust her ass in all those engineering classes? Finally, how can they expect to recruit women into engineering with this attitude still so prevalent? Attractiveness, like hairstyle, should not be assessed in engineers. "My hotness" should not have been considered. I was not treated as an equal, even though I was superior in education. I was in my 40s, and the year was 2019, not 1979.

I think this type of thing breeds imposters. It states in not-so-subtle terms that a woman will be viewed as an object, and that her "hotness" is what matters. She must therefore act in accordance with those dictates first—play a role and perform—which will only lead to feeling like a fraud.

I left my full-time job on August 6, 2019. I started a company based on the device I invented, which is controlled by Artificial Intelligence / Machine Learning (AI/ML). I learned all I could about computer engineering and business. But it was a little unsettling. I was working hard to sound like I was knowledgeable about these topics, even though I should have been OK with not knowing since they were not directly in my field. I was accustomed to being the expert in materials or testing. Trying to learn the business acumen needed as well as developing a product that required AI/ML was extremely challenging for me in multiple ways. I wanted to know and do it all. I worked more than needed and still felt like I had something to prove. I did not have business acumen, and I did not have a history in computer engineering. I felt insecure about my lack of knowledge, and I didn't like not being the expert. I was well outside my comfort zone.

I wasn't comfortable not knowing things, but even when I admitted to myself I didn't know something and asked questions, I was labeled with imposter syndrome, not just curiosity. This label came from the people who were considered experts in accelerating businesses. Why, when I asked questions, was the label "imposter syndrome" assigned? Questions are normal, and doubt is natural. As a society, let's agree that questions are good. Again, I am not an expert, and I do admit I have imposter syndrome—just not about computer engineering or business. Personally, when I am experiencing imposter syndrome, I don't ask questions. I pretend I know everything about the topic.

It was hard to admit that I had any issues when I was told I had imposter syndrome. I felt as though others, too, may have been labeled with self-doubt based on looks alone. The truth is, we all feel like a "fish out of water" sometimes—and that's OK. The focus shouldn't be on labeling insecurity and doubt; it should be on helping people get the skills and confidence they need to go forward with curiosity and vulnerability.

Stepping out of my comfort zone had the side effect of making me confront issues in myself and in our society. I want to focus now on solutions.

Sitting at tables can be easy or uncomfortable. I have sat at tables where I knew I belonged, but my presence was not welcome—nevertheless, I knew I had the expertise and made my voice heard. What I really want is to sit at tables where I am welcomed, even if perhaps I do not belong, because I want to impart wisdom or have wisdom imparted on me. I hate that there are groups of people who have been excluded from tables and whose voices have not been heard.

Imposter syndrome manifests itself in very different ways in different people. In my case, imposter syndrome affects me in instances where my personal behavior differs from the expected normal "womanly" behavior. It wasn't until I was exposed to the concept of imposter syndrome that I realized that my aversion to holding babies and feelings of inadequacy in groups of women were actually symptoms of my own imposter syndrome. Conversely, the "diagnosis" of imposter syndrome that I received regarding my business venture proved to be inaccurate. It was based on false assumptions regarding the questions that I asked to increase my understanding of business and computer programming. These assumptions were based on people's preconceived ideas about my level of understanding and my self-confidence. The reality is that I ask questions to increase my knowledge, and to ensure that I feel like I deserve a seat at the table.

My Own Imposter Syndrome: Babies and Groups of Women

It is difficult to deal with insecurities, even in my mid-forties. It is amazing how much I don't like to think about the things I am not good at, or about myself. First, let me address the baby thing.

I don't dislike babies—in fact, I am drawn to them. I like their purity—how un-self-aware they are, how funny. I would say I like, even, *love* babies and children. However, I do not love holding babies—and I resent the assumption that I would want to.

Of course, if a situation dictates that a child must be held and there is a shortage of hands, I can and will do it—just like, if needed, I would jump on a grenade—but too often the assumption is made that based on my sex and perhaps my age, that I would *want* to hold an infant, and so a baby is thrust into my arms, instead of into the arms of my husband or my male cousin, both of whom are far more accustomed and comfortable with small children and babies than I am.

As mentioned, I don't like to be bad at things. I especially do not like to be made to feel inadequate at things that are deemed by society or nature or whatever something I should be good at and enjoy. One hundred percent of the babies I have held have stiffened and cried. They seem to not enjoy being held by me, and I do not want to be made to feel inadequate.

When I started writing this book, I was convinced I didn't have imposter syndrome. But upon some self-reflection, I became aware that, yes, I did have imposter syndrome, but not in the way it was "assigned" to me. It is a monster that can manifest itself in a myriad of ways.

I am the youngest of eight children. As my mom was the youngest in her family, I am therefore the youngest of my many first cousins as well. My siblings had children but they lived far away and I saw them rarely. My oldest sibling with children didn't think I was very competent, and once said to me as a child, "Do not drop her, or I will never forgive you." Looking back, I am certain this didn't help the situation, but I don't think it can be the cause. My hesitation around babies didn't start with my older sister. Maybe it's simply that I was never thrust into the position where a baby was in my care. Of course, I would never intentionally harm a baby, but they do seem fragile, and well, diaper changing is just gross. My husband has changed more diapers than I have, a fact I do not envy. I am pretty certain that I have changed one or maybe two diapers in my life, I don't know, but the grenade I mentioned earlier sounds about as appealing.

When I got out of the Army, one of my sisters needed help watching her children—to date they were the youngest children I have cared for long-term. My niece was two at the time and probably has memories of me that illuminate how unaccustomed I was to dealing with smaller children. Personally, I remember a time where she was very upset that her older brother was teasing her, and she waddled over complaining to me. She was mumbling and I couldn't understand her, so I said, "Go compose yourself and then come back to me and tell me what is wrong." She was two years old. Not surprisingly, she didn't come back, nor would she. I just didn't understand that this was not the way to deal with a toddler.

In general, I don't talk down to kids. As the youngest around, I was usually talked down to, and I hated it. I swore to never do it, which is why I speak to kids like equals. That being said, I understand now that although you should not talk down to children, there are so many things that are different in a child's mind. Time management, for instance: they have very little understanding of this concept, which isn't all that surprising considering they exist in a world where birthdays take forever to come and "grownups" are in the 6th Grade. Anyway, over time, I've grown to understand their limitations better and have adjusted. And the truth is children like me: I don't talk down to them or use a dumb baby voice, and I often seek their wisdom on Nerf guns and toys.

I do know that I should not be in charge of what kids watch. I once took my young nephew to see a movie when he was six or seven that was rated PG-13. I knew not to take him to see R-rated movies, but aside from this I didn't pay much attention. I sat next to him as inappropriate joke after inappropriate joke was told and cringed, thinking my sister would kill me if she ever saw the movie. Afterwards, I told my nephew that he could never let his mom see "Talladega Nights: The Ballad of Ricky Bobby." It has been 17 years— my nephew is now in his 20s—and I'm pretty sure my sister still has not seen that movie. He still talks about how awesome it was to see that movie in the theater with me.

In many ways, watching my sisters' kids exposed me and helped me to move past some of my issues caring for young children, but they were young children, not babies. I have not been around babies for a long period of time, and honestly that's fine with me. I would like to think, if it was needed of me, I would do it, but it's not something I would choose to do, and I hate the assumption I would want to.

As I've gotten older, I have dug my feet in. I resent the assumptions that are made, many of which seemed to be based on my sex. I hate that people think that just because I'm a woman, I would be competent in the role of watching a young child. Just because I have XX Chromosomes should not indicate that I want to hold your damn baby. And that you have the expectation is insane and, frankly, sexist. Ironically, women themselves are by far the worst offenders in this arena. Instead of making me feel like it is OK to not want to have those instincts, I am constantly told "I can" without the slightest consideration of if "I want to." If one chooses to have a baby and care for children—great, I do not make any assumptions about that job. I chose a different path, and I would like that to be honored as MY CHOICE. I don't need a pep talk about what I CAN DO. I know these encounters are not ill-intentioned but that doesn't mean they are not offensive. I feel like the same culture that says this is what an engineer "looks" like dictates that I "look" like I would want to hold a baby. And this shallow, outdated perspective has made me feel like an imposter, because I simply am no good at what I "look" like I'm supposed to be good at. Intellectually, I know I will not get better at it if I don't expose myself—but for some reason, I am terrified of exposing myself in this arena. I can't even seem to ask any questions.

I love all my siblings, but I was especially close to my sister Brigid, who was nearest in age to me. She was able to choose to stay home with her children. She thought it was a great complement to tell me I would make a great mom someday. I never told her that was not my plan, that I truly believed I was meant for other things. I can help people a great deal more with the Upward Mobility and Buswell Biomedical. She died suddenly, and her body was discovered by her son. When she died, I didn't know how to deal with her children, who were all teenagers at that time, but I tried to provide them with what I would want: love and respect. I am certain she would have done a better job, but in so many ways I was never her—we chose different paths.

I always thought I would be able to draw on her expertise on children and makeup. (She, on the other hand, would turn to me when she needed help picking out car tires.) I had a full-on mascara meltdown the other day, and Brigid was the one I would have called to ask for advice. I miss her so much. I used to get mad about how long she spent in the bathroom getting ready while I waited either for her or the bathroom. Now I wish I spent a little more time trying to understand what she was doing in there. Perhaps I would not be filled with anxiety and fear choosing mascara if I had asked her more questions like this.

My deal with women is similar to babies—however, women make up half the population: it's harder to avoid them. I now work out at a women-only gym called "Dragonfly Fitness," and I have been so lucky to get to know great and powerful women in my life in general. My grandma, for instance, was a real badass. Born in 1901, she lived through WWI, the Spanish Flu, the Great Depression, WWII, her husband dying of Cancer at a relatively young age, Vietnam, and the Cold War. She saw both her sons drafted and when my dad deployed when my mom was pregnant with the seventh of eight kids, Grandma moved from NYC to a small desert Army base in Utah to be with my mom, and lived with us for as long as I can remember. She died in 1995. She is the one who asked me the wonderful question that always helps to put things in perspective: "Will this matter in a year?" I was in third grade and my best friend said she didn't want to be my best friend anymore. Understandably, I was upset at the time, but my Grandma was correct: it didn't matter in a year.

Women are people and I know this, but there are aspects of women that intimidate me in a way I can't articulate. I recently went to this gym and participated in conversation after over a year. It took me that long to simply realize that I have a lot in common with these women and we have shared experiences. So instead of just observing them, I interacted and talked to them.

Aside from the scenario above, I am simply ill at ease with women in general. I like to think I am brave, but honestly groups of women scare me. I am intimidated and I feel insecure. I feel separate from their world—a world of make-up, shopping, grace, and well-groomed hair. My hair seems to stick up in strange ways, and my makeup always looks like it was ill-applied by a child.

I am 46 years old and mostly gray; I hate that when I think of coloring my hair, it scares me. I wish my hair wasn't gray, but I hesitate to dye it. I feel like there is an expectation to not go gray naturally as a woman, but also there is an expectation to know about this stuff, and I hate it all. I know this is societal, but I think of Mighty Mouse when I see men who color their hair. I am judgmental about it, but in truth I am envious—I feel like they can go gray so they should.

Similarly, I wear makeup when I go out. My sister says she "wears makeup for herself." I definitely do not wear makeup for myself, but I feel the expectation to wear it so I conform. As I age my eyelashes and eyebrows are disappearing and I feel I should know what to do about it. My husband has the same situation (well he isn't gray), but he simply moves on. He knows what he has to offer the world isn't tied to his appearance. I know this, too, and yet somehow I still find myself succumbing to these outdated systems of thinking. The truth is I am not great to look at, never was, and I have always been told that is not what is important. Yet messages like aging men are "distinguished," while aging women are "old" reinforce the idea that this nonsense *is* important. At the very least, these messages imply I should know about hair and makeup.

The more I don't know about things, the more I am intimidated by those who do know—at least when it comes to women and babies. In business and computer engineering, I had no problem seeking out the experts and asking them questions. With hair and makeup, I don't ask—I simply pretend. I "act" like I fit in those spaces, even though the truth is I feel apart. I have let my insecurity around these groups take hold and make me an imposter.

To practice overcoming my insecurities, I have purposely put myself in places where I am surrounded by women. I now belong to a yoga studio where most of the members are women. I also joined a Women Strength Building Gym. The truth is, I go to many things where I am surrounded by women specifically. But this has not made me feel different. I still don't ask questions, but I do not assume all women are secure in these abilities, either. Who says they've all spent the ten thousand hours required to be an expert in makeup? I may have been assuming these women are all the same, and that, too, is unfair. This false assumption—that all women must somehow feel at ease doing "girly things"—may be part of what perpetuates this sense of imposter syndrome in myself.

I want to make clear that it isn't that I think women are weak. My Mom is incredibly strong, and she looks like Elizabeth Taylor and knows about makeup. I have been surrounded by strong beautiful women that are smart and do not appear to have the same hang ups. Or maybe they do have the same hang ups and they simply do not speak about them? I do not know.

I would like objectively to have all the things that come with being a man, including standing up to pee. I think penises are silly—at times they make me laugh—but it would honestly be nice to not have to squat and bare my ass to pee. Also, I'd rather not have to have the same interactions with the gross bathrooms as is currently necessary.

The other thing that would be nice about being a man is not having to worry about dying my hair or wearing makeup. Of course, men have to deal with prejudices when it comes to all this, too—and honestly, I think it's crap that men get judged if they do dye their hair or wear makeup. Can we simply agree as a society that these judgments are dumb and outdated?

Choosing to change yourself is always the best way to ask society to change. Me, I am putting myself in rooms filled with other women that I would historically avoid. I even have an appointment to put a gloss on my hair—I have not picked a color, although I am leaning towards the yellow hues. I am making progress, and I am trying to give myself grace, but in spite of all my efforts, I often still feel uncomfortable. But that's OK.

Everyone fears something: for me, it's babies and makeup; for other women, it's math and mechanics. Isn't it time we stop judging each other for what we fear and lack expertise in? Isn't it time we stop pointing out each other's weaknesses? In the end, we all experience doubt in some arenas—which is part of what makes us similar, and part of what makes us human. Perhaps we can find a certain strength in the fact that we are all, at times, weak. Maybe we can all share this, exchange it, and come out stronger on the other side. I know I do not apply makeup well—help me with it, please. I will help you with your math.

CHAPTER TWO

THANK YOU FOR YOUR SERVICE

By Stacey Brown

Editor's Note: Stacey and I got to know each other through Entrepreneurship Bootcamp for Veterans. We initially met virtually, and spoke several times online, but I only knew her from her photo. When we finally met in person at the camp, she was a talented person whom I enjoyed spending time with.

Would I still have a job if I didn't deploy?

I remember the day it started; I legitimately felt like a fraud. Fifty days into my new role as a sales supervisor of a Fortune 100 company, I was tasked with presenting a year-end review. I'd been an account manager with this company previously, but the position had dissolved while I was on a military assignment. When I learned about the dissolution, I was worried, afraid, and heartbroken. So much of my identity had been intertwined into my career. *What am I going to do now?* I wondered.

Because my leave of absence was to fulfill military service, I was fully entitled to reemployment with the same company once I returned. Only, now the closest opportunity was two states away! This presented quite a dilemma. However, in less than three months, human resources phoned me regarding an impending opening. I swiftly answered the call in the same manner I would approach any fight or flight scenario: I prepared to put my best foot forward!

Interviewing for a position when I had no idea what it entailed wasn't unusual for me. I've always had a natural curiosity. This natural curiosity led me to research the unknown and study statistics ad nauseam. This ensured I had answers for the 5 W's & H (who, what, when, where, why, and how). I assembled infographics detailing my plans to make an immediate impact. I proudly displayed a record number of awards, achievements, and customer reviews. No interview would be complete without having a few questions prepared for the interviewer. My high school basketball coach taught me this level of over-preparedness. "If you push harder in practice," he told us, "the game will be easy for you." He was right! Practice was often intense, as we vied for every point, position, and possession. His "outwork your opponent" philosophy was successful. It led us into a 31-0 championship season. So, I wanted to make it work for me in this interview, too.

With memories of past successes firmly in mind, I confidently arrived at the interview. My presentation was printed, and my cover letter and resume were protected. I was dressed in a tailored suit, ready to reclaim my position in management. I aced the interview, and within only a few days I was welcomed into the new role.

The honeymoon lasted only a few microseconds. Customers were unforgiving, management was condescending, and maintaining adequate staffing was an ongoing challenge. Seemingly, everywhere I'd turn, there was a fire to put out. Every time the phone rang, my presence was needed. The deluge of emails, phone calls, meetings, and traffic became my norm. I couldn't keep up. I quickly grew overwhelmed. I found myself buried in the trenches. I was deeply discouraged and conceded to my manager that I'd bitten off more than I could chew. He replied: "You've deployed to Afghanistan; this is nothing to stress."

I had become a shell of myself. I couldn't see how to get myself out of this rut. Working lunches took on a new meaning entirely. My car filled with pizza boxes, headache medicine, and water bottles. Employees were often unavailable, resulting in customers' needs going unmet. Micromanagers complained of lackluster sales. Down-time was an afterthought. Even sitting at home on my sofa with my company laptop in tow, I frequently dozed off as I struggled to compile daily reports.

Once the first month was complete, I was relieved to have gotten through it. Seemingly my peers were more skilled, though I reminded myself that there was a good reason for this: They had at least a one-year head start! I'd be as well-versed if given the same opportunities. So much for sulking.

I started my new role with the company November 18th. I was tasked with presenting the prior year's data on January 5th. Though I'd only had a little more than a month on the route, management's position was: "You inherit the problem."

This year-end review was my first real order of business. While my colleagues expressed their apprehension of public speaking, I felt confident. Mentally, I reverted to interview preparation. Sure, I hadn't been there long, but I could easily articulate a Strengths, Weakness, Opportunity, and Threat (SWOT) analysis. With the help of visual slideshow presentations, including Google slides, Prezi, & PowerPoint, I was able to put together a compelling report, highlight my territory's wins, as well as set attainable short-term goals.

Now for the moment of truth: It was time for me to present. Sure, I had some nerves, but nothing out of the ordinary. Sweaty palms, no appetite, cracking voice—these were all normal feelings that usually went away once I started. But this day was different. I was afraid to make eye contact, unsure of why I suddenly felt so intimidated. Though I'd practiced, you couldn't tell because somehow, my favorite filler word was now "um." As I spoke of plans of performance improvement, I heard competing voices in my head say things like "aren't we optimistic?" "What makes you think you can do xyz?" "Why didn't it work last month/year?" "Excuses, excuses, everybody has them." "Blah blah blah." I lost focus. I tried to project an energetic front, but in that moment, I would rather have been in absolutely any other place.

I ended with the statements: "My area's a mess. It needs a ton of work, but we'll get there. Are there any questions?" To further highlight the awkwardness, someone started a slow clap, which I took as my cue to disappear. I did so with great relief!

Months after the presentation, I was still taking the subpar delivery extremely hard. Managers and coworkers tried to offer support, but for the life of me I couldn't figure out why I'd bombed so bad. Had I just been fooling everyone, including myself? Was I really incapable of delivering on my promises? After a lifetime of success, why did I now feel like I was no longer good enough? Had I just been skirting by all this time?

I took these concerns and sought professional help. The adviser observed my experiences were imposter syndrome, which can manifest in many forms—namely, the perfectionist, natural genius, soloist, and expert. In my case, I portrayed the superhero. Superheroes feel like they must excel in all different roles, and so they have the tendency to push themselves past their limits. Admittedly, he was right. Throughout my life as a civilian, I had always been self-motivated, easily adaptable, and a high achiever. However, the military was an altogether humbling experience. It helped me understand the pain of being picked last, or not picked at all. It helped me understand the disappointment of having my qualifications questioned, as if meritorious achievement doesn't apply. I understand life is not fair and, in many environments, I'm expected to work twice as hard for half as much recognition. Is it sobering? Yes! But then I realized I needed to give myself grace.

Well-intentioned as that year-end presentation may have been, there was no doubt it was a colossal failure. I think I may have even cried—and if I didn't, I certainly wanted to. The gravity of just how much work needed to be done hit me, and as I stood in front of my expressionless peers, I had never wanted to disappear so badly. But something powerful evolved from that nightmare moment. I began investing in myself.

I started setting boundaries, which meant working no more than eight hours during the weekday. It meant taking dedicated lunch breaks, minus phones and computer interruptions. Most importantly, it meant asking for and receiving help.

Prioritizing my mental health has done wonders for my psyche, and journaling frequently helps me document and celebrate the good. I spend less time ruminating on the bad. I have come to grips with the idea that, though I didn't blow that presentation out of the water, my vulnerability had raised awareness with upper management, showing them they needed to invest in their people. I may have lacked proper resources and training, but that has never made me less worthy. As a woman, a leader, and an innovator: *I. Am. Enough.*

CHAPTER THREE

PLAYING VARSITY

By Kate Mansker

Editor's Note: Kate and I met in 2005. We both worked at the same place at that time. Kate is driven and smart. She was my running buddy, and we also have been known to go to weddings together. We danced, and when we didn't like the music, we simply went to another reception. We knew each other when we were single and struggling to find our place. In the end, we attended each other's weddings, too, and I am so proud to call her my friend.

A t 22 years old, I dove headfirst into my career with a chemical engineering degree tucked under my arm. My first job out of college was at a two million square-foot facility with over 2,000 employees. Hard hats and steel-toe boots were required. There was a hierarchy of roles delineated by hard hat color. General employees wore white hard hats. The technical services department wore orange hats, and maintenance wore yellow. Blue was reserved for management. I took diligent notes during orientation and was eager to get things started until I received a hard, blue hat. Blue?! I didn't even know where the bathrooms were. There must be some mistake: I wasn't qualified to wear a hard blue hat!

In retrospect, my rookie demeanor was undeniable. Nobody was asking me where the bathroom was. Among the thousands of employees, newbies were easy to spot regardless of hard hat color. I would soon learn this.

A typical forty-year career was once described to me as four ten-year segments, each categorized by the familiar monikers of freshman, sophomore, junior, and senior. I have found this depiction to be strangely accurate. It captures the mindsets common while in each of those career phases. Freshmen are wide-eyed and new to everything. Sophomores are a little self-assured but still learning. The sophomores and juniors generally run things, but the juniors have a little grey hair. The seniors are a wealth of knowledge but tend to be a little aloof to the hustle gripping the rest of the school. They are eyeing graduation, also known as retirement. This is a vast generalization, but the tendency is there.

While at the plant, I was assigned to assist with an aggressive energy-saving initiative. There were top-notch consultants brought in and fancy spreadsheets created to correlate energy usage to production. This was a language I understood from my prior years as an engineering student and intern. We learned that corporate directors planned to tour the operational changes that resulted from our plant's initiative. I poured myself into the spreadsheets that had been created to make sure I understood them well enough to explain them to our visitors. For extra panache, I ordered a collared shirt with the company logo from the company store on my own dime. I was still new, but I wanted to sound and look professional. The tour went well, and I was beginning to learn what it took for me to feel like I belonged, was qualified, and was truly contributing.

Halfway through my freshman career phase, I started a family. This was common for my age group, but I would soon learn that being a new mom versus a new dad in the workplace held significant differences. Until that point, I had not faced much adversity in being female. In engineering school and at work, there had been lots of other females in addition to several wonderful mentors, both male and female. I was the beneficiary of the glass ceiling breakers and trail-blazers before me. Also, I've always worked in technical fields where willingness to learn and problem-solve were valued over superficial traits. Alas, I finally hit a snag when I tried to get breastmilk through airport TSA while traveling for work. I traveled with a breast pump, called hotels ahead of time to make sure I had access to a freezer, and pumped in family restrooms at convention centers. Logistically, I figured out how to make it work with some errors along the way. I am happy to report that TSA eventually caught up to the basic concept of mammals.

However, it became apparent to me why many women exit the workforce when they have kids. The environments and resources are improving, but there is still logistical friction in accommodating excellent women in the workforce who happen to be parents. Seeing other women and mothers in the workforce has become even more important to my own journey. If I can see other women and parents navigating the rough seas, I know it's possible. Not easy, but possible. Since it was difficult to get through airport security as a nursing mother without my child, I questioned my role and if the work travel was worth the hassle. These were the moments when I realized how easy it is to feel like an imposter.

Being a working parent was the impetus to look for ways to eventually work for myself. The opportunity to do so arrived later in the sophomore phase of my career. I started an engineering firm with my brother. We were both in front of clients signing contracts and in front of the banker signing loans. I was in new territory, and I was stressed. We poured money into the endeavor, hoping it would yield revenue. I needed to portray a sense of leadership and experience, but at thirty years old, I still looked young. In the engineering field, youth is synonymous with inexperience. Many people lament grey hair, but I actually wanted more of it. I wanted to look the part, like purchasing a "logo-ed" shirt before my presentation to corporate at my first job. My brother and I were discussing our prospects and strategies when he used a term that captured my scenario perfectly. He said, "Yeah, you look young, but you are a starting sophomore." I knew exactly what he meant, and it was a huge compliment. From our high school days, typically, juniors and seniors make the varsity team. Occasionally, you get a sophomore or two or maybe a really good freshman who makes the varsity team and even starts the game. You show up to practice, you hustle, you work hard, and you cooperate as a team. So, when the coach tells you that you'll be starting the game on Friday night, you don't forfeit the opportunity based on some limiting belief. Others are working hard and would love to start the game. Even more importantly, others have forged the path so that you can even play the sport.

When I first heard about imposter syndrome, it sounded similar to what I considered an underclassman might experience playing varsity. The more I came to understand imposter syndrome, the more I realized that it focuses on a single moment in time, a feeling. Feeling unsure, self-doubt, like a fraud. But feelings eventually change like weather patterns. Situations change, too. Those selling solutions to imposter syndrome tend to focus on a common insecurity. The universal uncertainties that come with trying something new. A new school, a new job, a new town, a new industry, a promotion. Who am I to think that I deserve to be here? In my experience, self-doubt indicates there is meaning and significance in the challenge ahead of me. It is human nature to question the path when things get uncomfortable. And if you are a female, a person of color, or neurodivergent, there can be lots of uncomfortable moments in the workplace. The system and its traditions were built by a very narrow segment of the population. Challenging and changing workplace norms can be difficult, but also immensely important, even vital. Employers need to actively create workplace cultures that appeal to today's workforce. Refusing to do so is a quick way to a company's demise. I often return to the idea of being a sophomore varsity starter in these situations. It rounds out the sharp but fleeting pang of self-doubt. The idea of being a freshman or sophomore on the varsity team has underlying messages that motivate me and put things in perspective:

- You will be going up against people with more experience than you; this is how you learn.

- Let your opponents underestimate you; that can work in your favor.
- You made the cut to be on varsity for a reason—focus on your craft.
- You are part of the team—help your teammates and lean on them when needed.
- You bring the vigor and stamina that the older generation tends to have in limited supply.

Currently, I'm starting the junior phase of my career. I still have much to learn, but I am finally sporting more of the grey hair that I wanted years ago. Even though I have more experience, I still encounter new situations with occasional self-doubt. If I look beyond those feelings, I can focus on the significance and meaning of the challenge. I cherish my family and the opportunity to run a fulfilling business and career. I appreciate the progress others have made so that I can participate in this capacity. It was challenging for the first women to work as engineers or the first mothers to have careers. They overcame a lot to carve out the opportunities I have. One of the greatest opportunities I now have is to put into effect the changes needed in the workplace. It is a great honor to hire excellent people with diverse backgrounds and varying levels of experience. Even though I may be the coach at times, I still play varsity, suiting up in steel-toe boots and a hard hat.

CHAPTER FOUR

INGRID THE IMPOSTER

A CAREER PATH LIKE CHUTES AND LADDERS

By Ingrid Weissenfluh

Editor's Note: Ingrid Weissenfluh and I met as part of the Entrepreneurship Bootcamp for Veterans (EVB), which was held at the University of Connecticut. She waited for my much-delayed plane, and we met in the baggage claim area at the Hartford Airport. We talked in the car on the way to the hotel, and found we shared a lot of ideas and interests. Even though we were technically "linked" through the online "phase 1" portion of EVB, meeting her in person made such a big impression on me. She was a good friend to me when I ended up with COVID during the bootcamp, and we have remained in touch since.

Ingrid is smart and kind. She adds value to all the rooms she occupies; you are lucky if you find yourself at a table with her.

mposter syndrome is split into five categories: the perfectionist, the superwoman, the natural genius, the soloist, and the expert. Some theorists would have you believe that you can't be all the categories in a few hours. This is not true. Especially for me. Depending on the sequence of tasks and the added weight of naysayers, each phase is either as long and slow as the Mississippi River or as fleeting as a heartbeat. I first found myself to be an imposter because I got the idea in my head that I could break a perceived generational curse and realize success by being one of the first people in my immediate maternal lineage to complete college.

My challenge is to travel a path full of perils. Many people are born in small, impoverished towns and contend with desperate, no-hope situations. Even the most torrid of gothic drama authors could not convey their options. I will not try to do what they, in their brilliance, could not. Instead, I will simply try to tell the follies of traveling my own path.

I was a fair-to-good student in school. Still, like many, I had to focus in so many directions. Consistent academic excellence eluded me. I retook classes and changed my study techniques as often as I changed my major. I still made progress, but only in small increments. Completing one class and then the next was my only real accomplishment. This was my hard-won lesson: keep going forward, one course after another, even though it sometimes felt like a rhythm of failure. Although every board and developmental team made it a point to include me in their number, the assumptions of some smug professors often prevailed in influencing others that because I wasn't a good student, I was not worth help or consideration. I was in a program where if your grades weren't all A's, you had nothing to say. Time and time again, I was good enough to grind out the work, but never to get the grades that would mean scholarships and invitations to graduate studies.

Getting into the university was another hurdle that was not easy to clear. Of course, I was not alone in this: Each year millions of students will apply, and based on the guidelines of each school, they are either denied or admitted. Additionally, students who could not to afford the tuition are placed in order of merit, and based on my performance, I found that I would need student loans to fund my education.

I was armed with a strong constitution in junior college at the Mississippi Gulf Coast Community College, but I was distracted. I was balancing life, and it was unclear what my new dream of education would provide or how it would lead me towards my destination. In my mind, the traditional routes to becoming a doctor were closed to me. I didn't have high medical school entrance exam scores (MCAT) or money to force open the doors of a medical admissions office. Academic excellence was something I could not maintain. During those times, I did not think I was doing something hundreds of thousands of people would never even have the opportunity to attempt. Thousands more would enter the university halls, and thousands more would exit with no degree and massive debt, shackled to their now-buried dreams.

After six years, I held my bachelor's degree in Psychology from the University of Southern Mississippi in my hand. Still, I was not the best or the brightest, and I could not find a good job in my chosen field of psychology. I wasn't one of the lucky ones who had somehow managed to pull themselves out of a desperate situation and break the cycle that's repeated too often throughout our country, but that's repeated even more frequently in Jackson County, Mississippi—one of the poorest counties in the most impoverished state in the USA.

I had to devise a way to be worthy of any accomplishment. I was now a state employee—the goal for some peer groups—and I may have been in a new room with slightly more light, but I still felt like I was in the back of a line populated with people I knew were all more accomplished. I was learning about an even more exclusive plateau of existence. I felt again as I did when I started my college journey—like a liar and imposter in a room full of people who had moved beyond the hallowed halls of academia into careers of substance and skill. Me, I had just slipped through, as if no one had been watching the door.

I found a way into what I thought was an exclusive club: a job working in law enforcement for the Mississippi Department of Public Safety. I thought this was a safe place for a while. I could provide value and pay tribute for everything l had overlooked and done wrong in skipping stages that others had laid out as necessary. I worked at the lower rungs of state employment. Then, a glimmer of an idea came to me: attend the state law enforcement academy. I did what I thought was more than enough to prepare for the grueling push of people and pain.

But again, I did not quite reach the mark. I failed the academy. All the while, I thought of how I had stolen everything. Somewhere out there was a better candidate who would have passed the test, and I had taken their place or opportunity.

I continued at the lower rungs, which was where I thought I belonged. I had stolen an opportunity to attend the state patrol academy and failed miserably. This didn't stop me, but I still didn't feel like l belonged. I skulked back into my books, and the safety of my little state office. I worked and punished myself. I needed to have routines, and I studied to increase my capacity and veracity. I was told, even in print, that I had taken the place of a young man who would have been successful. I knew then that maybe I was the better candidate, and that opportunities do not necessarily have to be completed to be successful. I had learned to move beyond the assumptions of everyone who said I was not the best choice. I now felt I didn't have to be the best choice—only my own choice. I still could not manage to congratulate myself—but I had begun to take consistent strides toward my own goals. Going forward, I did more than look to be the best—I began to believe that I should be the one to bet on to win. A change in words, yes, but even more, a momentous change in personal ethos.

I came across a chance to work as a state law enforcement officer in the Department of Transportation. Once I arrived at the academy entrance, I knew this was a door I could either walk through or slink away from to return to my quiet office and books. I slipped through the door, returning week after week for more of the same persistent challenges. First, I spent days failing, listening to others laugh at the ease of the daily training tasks and added physical activity. It was not as rigorous as military training but all the same it was designed to build group cohesion and ease the path to compliance. I started in the middle of the pack of physically prepared candidates and worked my way up to the front. I tried hard to move on, but there remained in me a feeling like I had lied, like maybe I had taken something from someone else. The imposter in me continued to stare back at me daily. By this point in my life, I had collected three degrees, and I was diligently working on two others, but I still felt insufficient, like an imposter who'd slipped into the room when no one was looking. I wasn't my own best choice for success. I could not pick me first for any team. And I wanted to not feel like what you were left with, but what you chose.

Another chance to prove myself?

The Army was the furthest point from academia I could go. There I could prove I had skills, because the Army would only give me acknowledgment for what I earned.

I walked into the office wanting to give. It was 2008, and the grinder that was the nation's war campaigns needed willing bodies to keep it going. I should have accepted the initial offer of enlistment. Commission was a complex and long-fought-for achievement. In my head, my imposter told me that I wasn't even good enough for that. It said, "You are standing before others to lead and withstand the scrutiny and the weight of their fates. You aren't sincere in your intentions; just leave the office." The imposter told me my lie would be exposed, and I would never hold the commission of Second Lieutenant in my hand.

In my journey, I would end up being chosen from a group that was less than one percent of one percent of every person in the country. If that was not enough, what was? I was now a leader, mentor, and coach—not only chosen, but sought out, too. I was somewhere, but this still was not quite enough.

On a day in July of the same year, I stood in a room before a young Army Captain. At the time, I thought this Captain was a giant among people. There I raised my right hand and swore to defend the Constitution of the United States against all enemies, foreign and domestic. What was I thinking? If I were lucky, I would fail the training anyway and end up in a truck driving old boots and tires around in Iraq.

I drove myself down to Georgia to a weathered military base and barracks riddled with asbestos tiles and mold. Fort Benning was and is a crucible of a place. I signed myself into the infantry school. No, I was not one of the first graduates, nor would I be the last. Still, women and men who had joined the reserve and received a commission during this time shared this experience. These courageous people went to Fort Benning, GA, to learn the Army Officer's tactics and baseline. I read and reviewed the tan pages of my blue-bound officer's handbook, and still, I couldn't quite get a handle on the basic skills. I stayed up weekends and bugged my successful classmates. They were worthy of their places and generous in showing me what I was doing wrong. I was admonished and tutored by grizzled staff sergeants, who knew better than to allow me to get past these challenges too easily. They took pity on me, and I was re-trained until somehow, I was leading my classmates and volunteering for more tasks, all thanks to the diligence of those instructors and my battle buddies—a new name but one that would go forward with me the rest of my life.

I struggled to learn the language of the Army. I struggled with all the things that maximized combat power. Though I'd made great friends, I realized that even then, I was an imposter. I had not known combat. I was merely a member of a privileged group. I saw the glimmer of a brighter future but was still standing on my tiptoes as my marginal graduation pushed me toward my unit.

I reported on an auspicious day as the reserve unit was mourning the loss of a fallen soldier. I wasn't fully prepared for the rules and expectations. I waited in the corner, emulating the behavior of my fellow soldiers. I soon was handed my next opportunity. I assisted in the planning of Operation Unified Response. The summarized mission was to rebuild a nation after catastrophic natural disaster. Like many of the soldiers assigned to the mission, I had lived through Hurricane Katrina. We were eager to lend help to the island nation to bring the help that many felt they never received after the hurricane.

In addition to volunteering, many of the service members on the mission galvanized their communities to send additional assistance and personally shipped additional supplies. I slowly helped mesh the multitudes of forces into a responsive force for good and rejuvenation. After the destruction of what was left of Haiti, particularly Port Au Prince, I was, again, confronted by the imposter in the mirror. I was a partial conduit of information. The contracted assistance only spoke Spanish and the Haitians on site knew only Creole French and broken English. I knew enough French and Spanish and coordinated the requirements to our team in English. I was then mistaken for someone introspective and skilled. I was a humanitarian? No, to me I was just one among a group, a single part of a much greater whole. Our group was part of a collective effort, but we were fortunate enough to find that our command was awarded the superior unit citation. Oddly enough, for me, it was another stolen moment. I still felt I hadn't given enough to earn it with my sacrifices, but I also knew it wasn't true that I hadn't done anything worthwhile. I threw myself back into study and found myself in the executive officer position.

Still, I could not truly lead until I went on a "real" deployment at the behest of well-meaning leaders and senior soldiers. This turned out to be Afghanistan in 2012, where I saw the aftermath of the burning of Korans, riots in prison, and insider attacks at the Ministry of the Interior.

This was when I became quickly desensitized. I no longer startled at the sound of alarms. I merely checked that my rounds were ready for the impending ground attack the loudspeakers reminded everyone about. I was then sent home with a pat on the back and metals to prove it. I wasn't anything at all; I returned to my life of books and boundaries. I had vacillated between all five categories of imposter syndrome many times. I was weathered and weary, and in spite of all the things I did to prove my value, no better for the experience.

Then I broke. I sat down one day and finally said, "I am enough. I'm me, that's all." I accepted that I had accomplished all of the lofty goals that I'd set for myself. All of the people who said what I was doing was improbable and impossible, I had proved them wrong.

I had been miserable for what seemed like ages. Then one of the people I met in training came to me one day and thanked me. I didn't know why. They told me it was because I had been someone who listened to them and had given them a chance. They said, "I hadn't met anyone like you, someone so unsure, odd, and determined all at once. But you told me to lead the way, and I did it." This situation began to happen to me more often. I would get a letter or an email. And repeatedly it was to thank me. I was no longer a liar or imposter during those moments and the days after. I was just me, and I was happy about it.

I won't say that I have conquered my imposter syndrome. I still shift through the phases, but my once uneasy feeling is now a comfortable part of me because I know that on the other side is me. I'm already standing there. It's a road full of pivots, turns, serpentines, and cha-chas, but your destinations are wherever you decide they are.

Go forward and explore the road.

CHAPTER FIVE

AM I REALLY A DUCK?

THE DANGER OF IMPOSTER SYNDROME DURING A CAREER CHANGE

By Peter Smith

Editor's Note: Peter Smith and I went to the same yoga studio. We became friends over time. He is smart and funny. We talked about work very little, and I have now known him for over ten years. His contribution provided insight I didn't have. Peter is the only man who responded to my request for content for this book. And he had a unique perspective to share, since he was an instructor of students in the field of nursing, as well as a working nurse at the time we met.

remember my first nursing class—how completely out of place I felt. I was surrounded by learners much younger than myself who had past experiences in some manner of medical profession or in the health care environment, whereas my previous skills centered on advertising and communications. I had excelled, enjoying a fulfilling career both financially and personally. However, in my late thirties, I realized the business arena was not where my true focus lay. I had always harbored a passion for medicine and retained a strong acumen for nursing. At 38 years old, I made the decision to change my career and pursue a baccalaureate degree in nursing. When I first attended nursing class, I was physically prepared with books, pens, paper, etc.— but psychologically, I felt like an imposter.

I thought my earlier professional experiences would guide me through my new scholastic endeavor. Yet even with all the knowledge, skills, and aptitudes I brought with me to my nursing program, I felt it was only a matter of time before I was labeled a fraud, and people would think I was inept at all things related to my new profession. External factors—like the faculty, administration, and staff all assuming I was already experienced due to my sex and age—were also fueling my internally perceived fraudulence. They showered me with continued praise and assumptions of future success, confident that earning my bachelor's degree in nursing would be accomplished with ease. These assumptions followed me into the hospital setting, as well, when I performed my initial clinical experiences. Even though I was donning the nursing student uniform, I was looked upon as either the doctor, the health care provider, or the clinician in charge—and all because I was a man of relatively advanced years. As a result, I found myself guiding the nursing students instead of being one of them— and this made me immensely uncomfortable.

As a student nurse, I studied intensely and maintained excellent grades. In part, of course, I did this in order to have the education necessary to provide safe and effective care to patients. However, I also studied fervently because I felt at any moment, it would be discovered I was not the expert in medicine everyone thought me to be.

Unfortunately, this typecast followed me into my first professional nursing position. Once again, because of my age and sex, assumptions were made I was a nurse with years of experience, even though this was far from the truth. I was brand new to nursing, yet others perceived I was a seasoned practitioner. Once more, I felt like an imposter. I remained ever fearful that at any moment I might make a mistake and others would realize I was not the expert they thought me to be.

During my first professional nursing position, I started to adjust my mentality. I began taking the initiative to inform others I was a new nurse—that I had studied hard and did understand nursing theory and practice, but that I was still a novice nurse and needed to perfect these skills, which required assistance from others. Several years passed before I became comfortable in my own nursing skin and no longer felt like a fraud.

Imposter syndrome comes under many titles: imposter phenomenon, fraud syndrome, perceived fraudulence, or imposter experiences. No matter what it's called, I still experience imposter syndrome almost daily in my academic position—though not as often—and I witness others enduring it, as well.

I have always been a high-achieving individual. Yet, despite my objective and subjective successes, I have often failed to internalize these accomplishments. There always seemed to be someone more knowledgeable or better in my field than myself. This oftentimes left me with self-doubt, feeling like I could not claim a professional space in my industry even though I had earned the right through my professional service, scholarship, and education. The fact that others often viewed me as exceptionally proficient because of my sex and age left me feeling less than competent. I was continually anxious about over-promising and under-delivering. Thus, I began employing the defense mechanism of minimizing my professional accomplishments so, in turn, others would begin minimizing their perceptions of my abilities.

As I evolved from a nursing clinician to nursing educator, I began to feel more and more competent at what I was doing. I began to see that my professional accomplishments were objective and measurable. By doing this, I was able to validate my successes and increase my confidence, allowing me to shed my imposter syndrome tendencies like water off a duck's back.

I still experience imposter phenomenon. But when I do, I now view the occurrence differently. I view it as an opportunity to reflect critically on the situation. For instance, when I feel afraid I might not be a good nurse educator, I reassure myself that this actually means I care about my students and their learning. Rethinking and reframing my mindset has increased my confidence and competence in a job I love.

So, am I a duck? Yes. I walk like a duck, talk like a duck, and act like a duck. This duck belongs at the table of nursing professionals and educators, and so does my voice and experience. I have earned the right to nest there, because I AM a duck … and not a fraudulent one as thought previously. I am confident I belong at the table.

CHAPTER SIX

OVERACHIEVING/ OVERWORKING

AN IMPOSTER SYNDROME JOURNEY

By Mary Imani

Editor's Note: Mary and I met through her younger sister, with whom I went to graduate school. Her sister is younger than me, but we have a similar background. Mary came to my house for my neighbor's 87th birthday party. We sat around a table and had dinner and have been friends ever since. Mary is a tough lady. She works hard—throwing herself fully into everything she sets her mind to—and she does a great job providing for herself.

One of the hardest things about struggling with the imposter syndrome is how alone the experience makes you feel. Sometimes misery loves company; simply knowing that we are not alone in this battle can help us survive it. Realizing that the feeling of being a fraud happens to others, too, may not help us completely overcome imposter syndrome, but it can help us take action. Once we have found support to motivate us, some of the actions we can take include going to therapy or studying what others have written about our situation. Simply talking to people who have experienced these same feelings can be incredibly valuable on its own as well.

My journey towards recognizing and dealing with imposter syndrome started not that long ago. You may be surprised that at the age of 49, I did not know anything about it. When Sheila asked me if I would like to be a part of her book, I immediately accepted. She explained that the theme of her book would be imposter syndrome or "self-doubt." After our first call, I started going through my memories to find a time that I experienced "self-doubt." I found plenty. During our second call, I described my story to Sheila and asked her opinion about the story that I'd picked. She paused, and I knew that something was not quite right. She explained very politely that the story was great, but I knew deep down that she was trying to tell me that it did not match her book's theme. I decided to start doing research about the topic.

After reading the published articles and blogs, I realized that despite all my achievements, I have grappled with feeling like an imposter whole my life. Even though the topic was very new to me, I knew then that I wanted to try to learn how to release myself from its grasp. Reading stories where people share their struggles with "self-doubt" has helped me realize that imposter syndrome is not an imaginary feeling;

it is an experience shared by many different people in many different circumstances. My hope is that, together, we can empower ourselves, overcome self-doubt, and advance confidently in our careers.

In the early studies that were done by Clance and Imes in 1978 (*Psychotherapy: Theory, Research & Practice, 15*(3), 241–247. https://doi.org/10.1037/h0086006), the main causes of imposter syndrome include family dynamics, cultural expectation, individual personality traits and comparison. Looking back, I believe that all these factors have played significant roles in my life.

I was born and raised in a middle-class family in a middle eastern country. My mom was a housewife, and my dad was a top manager in a social welfare organization. My mom was a very talented student in high school but could not continue her education. My dad had an associate degree in pharmacy, but he had to quit his studies and start working to support his younger brothers and sisters. I give this background to indicate that studying and being number one in my class was very important for my parents. During school, I was always studying hard to get top grades. In my dad's eyes, I was a failure if even the smallest mistake appeared in my homework. During the summer, I had to take extra courses to make my parents happy.

As I approached high school graduation, it only got worse. Entering the university was very hard as all the students had to pass an extremely competitive entrance exam—only 10% of the students could attend the university. As you may guess, my dad wanted me to be a doctor. While I was not accepted into medical school, I was admitted into pharmacy school, where I tried very hard and graduated as one of the top three students in my class.

Besides focusing on my university courses, I worked on improving my English and French, neither of which are native languages in m̅ country. I always thought that I needed to excel in whatever I did, so I worked very hard. But were my parents happy with these achievements? Of course not. Well, if I want to be fair, they were just a little bit pleased, but they still thought I should have tried to get a higher degree. I should add that pharmacy in my country is PharmD, which is a doctorate. The fact they were never satisfied no matter how much I achieved affected me as well. I was always thinking that I was not good enough, and so I felt I had to prove myself to everyone—especially my parents. The family expectation for success and perfection remains with me even now, many years after I grew up.

After two years working in a pharmaceutical company, I joined the Food and Drug Administration (FDA) of my country and worked there for ten years. In many countries like mine, science often mixes with politics, which is a terrible combination. I had to fight for science. This was the one time I had no self-doubt about what I was doing. Even though I was a hard-working scientist—maybe even a workaholic—I was threatened by a lot of higher managers and even the Minister of Health. But I believed the science was right, and for once in my life, it gave me the strength to fight for what I was doing.

One of my dreams had always been to move to US to study and work. As the pressures started rising at the workplace as well as in my personal life, I began applying to American universities, and eventually I was admitted to a master's program in chemistry with funding. Many people's initial reaction was to tell me that I was downgrading from a doctorate degree to a master's degree! I started thinking that maybe I was not good enough to be accepted into a PhD program.

After 13 years working as a pharmacist, I went back to school at the age of 37. I was studying in a new country with a different culture and a different language, and after so many years of not being in school, this was not an easy task. As a person with imposter syndrome immersed in a new environment, I encountered a lot of challenges, and often felt uncomfortable and out of place. My response to these challenges was to pour myself even more intensely into my work. My close friends called me superwoman. I finished my master's degree in one and a half years, publishing two papers from my research work. After graduation, I could not go back to my country, and I could not work here in the US. I had to do something. So, I started a PhD in chemistry, finishing the program with nine published papers and two patents. It was here at the end of my education that I reached a kind of breaking point: even though I had worked so hard and accomplished so much, I again started wondering who I thought I was, and what I had actually done. I could not stop questioning myself and my worth.

When I look at successful people around me, I imagine that their lives must be easy, and that they probably did not have to struggle to be successful like I did. Looking back, it always feels like everything that I've gained during my life has been done in the hardest way possible.

Now that I can identify imposter syndrome, I need to find helpful tips to combat it. I will try to set limits and boundaries to avoid being a workaholic. I will try to stop working too hard just so I can prove myself to my boss and my colleagues—and even to myself. I want to redefine success and praise myself for my efforts and achievements, even the small ones. I will remind myself that nobody is perfect.

It's easy to be hunted by imposter syndrome. But dear friends who may be suffering from self-doubt, there is a balance to be found.

CHAPTER SEVEN

NOT LETTING WHAT IS DONE TO ME DEFINE ME

RECOVERING FROM IMPOSTER SYNDROME

By Roseline Salazar

Editor's Note: Roseline Salazar and I were in Bunker Labs together. We were in the same cohort. I got to know Roseline and she helped me immensely. She met with me many times to discuss topics that are specific to engineering. She helped me to explain them so that they could be understood easily and not bore audiences. I met powerful people in that cohort, and I am glad for her particular help and influence.

"Aut viam inveniam aut faciam" is Latin for "I shall either find a way or make one."

Rosaline is a wonderful example of a human being who made a way for herself.

Growing up, I never felt like I was good enough. It seemed like I never did anything right, or I had to do things at least twice to get them right. Approaching my teenage years, I started building my self-confidence. I felt like I was heading the right direction. Graduation came and my parents were so proud of me.

I enlisted in the military when I turned 19. At 20, I was off to basic training. It was not a walk in the park, but I was confident that I could get through it and graduate. After all, I had strict parents who had taught me tough love. And it paid off; I finished basic training. Then after that I went on to my twelve-week technical school, graduated, and went on to my first base. I had an awesome sponsor who welcomed me with open arms. I was introduced to a bunch of airmen whom I befriended shortly after. Months passed, and one of my male friends was tasked to deploy. He signed a power of attorney for me to take care of his belongings, and then he left for his deployment location. And life went on as usual.

When he returned from his deployment, he took me to dinner. I did not know he had an ulterior motive. After dinner, he dropped me home and walked me into my apartment. Then he asked if he could hang out for a little bit. I brought out some soda for us then went to the restroom. I came back to chat with him, took a sip of my Pepsi and started feeling dizzy. Not long after, I saw his face above me and fell asleep. When I woke up, I felt this unbelievable pain down in my private area. I suspected the worst but told myself it couldn't be—he was a friend. So I let it be.

Three nights later, while at dinner, he said he had a confession to make and told me what I suspected all along. I was devastated. Feeling betrayed, I decided to turn him in. Due to the lack of evidence and witnesses—and to the fact this "friend" denied everything—the case was dropped. Not even my friends believed me, and I ended up losing them all. I felt alone. And even though I made new friends, life wasn't the same after that. I finally moved duty stations, which was a huge relief. This was my first experience that led to feelings of imposter syndrome, like I wasn't good enough to be alive, like I wasn't deserving of respect. My next experience would further cement that mindset.

After over five years of enlistment, my goal was to become an officer. I felt I could execute the duties of being a leader and manager. So once I graduated from my commissioning program, I completed the process. Fast forward: After ten years in the service, I was now a captain, deployed to a camp in Afghanistan. Things were great at first. I got to know my new team members, did some supply runs, and learned the ropes of the new job. About two months into my deployment, my boss became obsessed with me. He was also a captain but about to be promoted to major. He became incredibly possessive and would be jealous if I spoke to anyone but him. I was only allowed to be with my section workers. Over time, things got worse. He named specific people he didn't want me talking to. He also told the other members in the camp that I belonged to him, that he had first dibs. I wasn't allowed to talk to my own Air Force buddies, and they stayed away from me. At dinner, he would take me to the table for two so no one could join us. I felt trapped and suffocated. He dumped his work on me and blamed me for everything that went wrong, even though he wasn't doing his job at all. Everyone in the camp knew what was going on. Some brave people came to me and guided me into writing a harassment statement. I wrote a complaint and got an investigation launched. People who were on my side wrote statements in my favor. Waiting for that verdict was the longest four months of my life. I was confident that the judge would rule in my favor. I had witnesses, documentation, all my ducks in a row.

But when it ended, my case was deemed invalid. I had no lawyer to fight for me, and "my boss" was just given a slap on the wrist. He got to stay at the camp while I had to go. Everyone was upset because they knew he should have been the one to leave. So once again, I lost… I went to the higher leadership to ask for help. I was told that whatever happened to me was my fault because I allowed it to happen.

When the case was closed, we were able to head back to our home base in the US. I still felt in my heart that I wasn't done with this man for making my life a living hell. And I wasn't. I ran into the colonel who was the Air Force Inspector General for the Air Force Personnel in Afghanistan. He was also stationed at my home base. He told me, "Had I known then what I know now, I could have done more for you…" I told him, "Don't worry about it, I got it handled." He didn't know what I was talking about, but I had a plan.

Since the government didn't help me, I figured I would take matters into my own hands and write a book about what happened and how the people in power failed me. After giving it some thought, I decided not to write anything negative. Instead, I wrote about the steps I took—how I coped with my situations, how I moved on, and how I made my dream of writing a book come true. I did my research and talked to some good editors. I was excited about being able to write my first book. I based this book on facts and documentation from the investigation.

Then something happened. I experienced an intense wave of crippling self-doubt. Suddenly, I didn't feel worthy. I had lost both investigations. My head was telling me either it was the Military Justice system or me, and I knew I was correct—but how could I be believed over the government? Although everything I went through was real, I felt as if no one would believe me. I worried they would think I was just a female who tried to get two innocent males in trouble. I thought filing investigations would have brought justice, but that hadn't happened even though I had all the documents to support what I was claiming. I used coping strategies such as breathing and meditation to get through this rough time. But I was still unsure. I feared retaliation. I feared losing friends and family, but most of all, I feared being rejected by a publisher—that my book wouldn't be sold. Losing both investigations had led me into a state of depression, and now I was dealing with imposter syndrome, too: I felt like I deserved what had happened to me, like I was unworthy, and so was the story I had to tell.

But after a few sessions with my therapist, and after talking with some book coaches, I was assured I had nothing to fear. This was a wonderful thing to do. It would help others with imposter syndrome to come forward and tell their story as well. Now I was confident and ready to write this book.

As I continued to work on the book, waves of doubt resurfaced, and negative thoughts kept running through my mind. People might not believe me, and I might gain some enemies. But I pushed through. I told myself, I am going to do it. I sent my draft off to my editor who reassured me this was an awesome way to get my story across and make a difference. Others with this issue will realize it's okay to feel that way—that they're not the only ones, and that there are people who will support them. My book, *Make a Smooth Transition after the Military: Create Yourself a Wonderful Civilian Life* was self-published in July 2020. Once I held a printed copy, I felt proud of myself. The feeling of imposter syndrome was no longer with me.

CHAPTER EIGHT

A SEAT AT THE TABLE

I BELONG HERE

By Betsey Mercado

*Editor's Note: Betsey Mercado and I were also in the Veteran in Residence program
through Bunker Labs. We both know Roseline, and Betsey helped us each through
a difficult time. I have attended conferences where Betsey speaks, and she is eloquent and
intelligent. She is kind and gives good advice. Betsey is a strong person, and I would be
proud to sit at any table with her—especially if that table is in front of Congress.*

have spent most of my adult life volunteering. I've been a youth soccer coach. I've spent hundreds of hours in my kids' classes and at their schools, doing everything from helping make copies to building sets for their school plays. But perhaps one of my favorite volunteer roles was supporting the soldiers and families of the teams, companies, and platoons that my spouse led. Taking care of soldiers always felt so important.

As a military spouse, it was hard to decide on a career that would allow me to move from place to place. I got a degree in business administration. I continued volunteering. Organizations were hesitant to hire an employee that had an unpredictable schedule. A deployed spouse simply couldn't commit to long-term employment, so I continued to volunteer.

In 2016, I became a co-founder of the veteran tech nonprofit, Objective Zero Foundation. My many years of volunteer experience came in handy. I was able to offer a unique perspective on our mission and programs. The basic premise of the Objective Zero Foundation is to use mobile app technology to connect veterans to their peers to prevent suicide. We learned that the simple act of listening can save lives. Initially, our app was going to be only for veterans. After many discussions, we opened up to service members, their families, and caregivers. I know the importance of including families and loved ones as part of the solution.

With over 40,000 nonprofits in the United States, it is hard to break into the nonprofit space. I feel it's even harder to break into the veteran service organization (VSO) world, as many VSOs see other nonprofits as competition. Their philosophy is that we're all competing for the same funding and resources—some even think we are competing for the veterans themselves. In our early days, our team reached out to several fellow nonprofits in the veteran suicide prevention space. These other nonprofits had different programs and services than ours. We were set to discuss collaborations and partnerships. We offered to share our technology and innovate an upstream approach to suicide prevention. We were blown off, ignored, and flat out told that our idea and app would be a failure. Others had tried and failed, and we would be no different.

Major VSOs wrote us off from the beginning. Perhaps that was the point where the self-doubt and imposter syndrome started to creep in for me. Our team had no experience in the nonprofit world. We were a group of service members and veterans—and a military spouse—who were sick of losing our loved ones and friends to suicide. We weren't experts, but we were passionate about being part of the solution. So, we found an innovative approach: getting the military and veteran community connected to support and resources.

I knew I had many volunteer skills. I could recruit and manage volunteers to perform outreach. These skills were incredibly beneficial in our early days of setting up and growing our nonprofit. I went from the Director of Marketing to a co-Executive Director within a couple of years. I ended up taking over as a solo Executive Director after my co-director left the organization. I was representing Objective Zero at conferences, partnership discussions, and meetings. I was surrounded by people that had served, mainly men. There were many times I felt as if I didn't belong in the veteran nonprofit space. My perspective and presence was sometimes discounted and ignored. I can only speculate about whether that treatment was because I was a woman, a military spouse, or not a veteran. I simply didn't feel like I had a seat at the table.

I could be part of the same conversation with my team and outside stakeholders—I could even say the exact same thing as my male, veteran co-founders—and yet I would be ignored. If that doesn't create self-doubt, I don't know what could. I questioned what I had to offer our organization and if I was the right person to be the Executive Director. How far could commitment, passion, and dedication to the cause go if I wasn't a veteran myself? What could I do to improve our organization by myself as a leader?

For the first five years of our organization, nearly all the funds that were coming in were going directly into building the app and technology. No one was getting paid. I was a full-time volunteer Executive Director for several years. Surprisingly, many in the nonprofit space believed that our organization "wasn't serious enough" since we weren't paying anyone. I am not exactly sure how much more serious we could have been. We were so committed to our mission that we were willing to forgo a paycheck so we could support veterans. Let the imposter syndrome sink in again. Does my income, or rather my lack thereof, make me less of a leader or impact my ability to help others? We were able to help thousands of veterans and train hundreds of people in suicide prevention. Yet I couldn't shake the feeling that I wasn't doing enough, or that I was somehow doing it wrong.

I was once told by a fellow nonprofit leader to "fake it till you make it," and I've heard others echo that statement. I've never liked that thought process. In my line of work where lives are on the line, I cannot fake anything. I need to be honest and face the fact that I don't know it all—I must be vulnerable. I believe more in the concept of "fail fast and fail often." To test myself and my skills, I must just go for it and try new things. With a small, agile nonprofit we can quickly pivot if something isn't working—especially as technology is one of our core foundations. That change in thinking, including the decision to never try to fake anything, was a turning point for me.

I started a master's degree program with a human services focus and nonprofit concentration. I tried to stay on top of the latest research and news as it related to veteran mental health and suicide prevention. I used my newly formed grant writing skills to apply for more funding. I learned more about program evaluation and how to better communicate our impact. In my second year as Executive Director, we saw a significant increase in funding. We saw new opportunities for partnerships. We were also accepted into a tech accelerator. We saw an increase in app usage and volunteering through the Objective Zero App. We were selected for the Center for Disease Control and Prevention and CDC Foundation's Veteran Suicide Prevention Evaluation Project.

After six years of being a VSO co-founder, and over four years of leading the organization, I have learned many lessons. Perhaps the biggest of them all is that I do indeed have a seat at the table. My experience, knowledge, and voice is valuable, and I have made an impact. I think self-doubt will always find a way to creep in, but I have gotten past the point of wanting to prove myself to others. My actions speak for themselves. I have completed my master's degree, as well as three years of program evaluation with the CDC. I spoke on several panels on veteran suicide, and even testified before Congress. I will continue to focus on finding ways of increasing our impact. I will support others in the fight against veteran suicide.

Remember those VSOs that said Objective Zero would never amount to anything? We are now speaking at the same conferences as them. They are sharing the Objective Zero App to the veterans they serve as another resource, and we're now seen as peers.

CHAPTER NINE

A PLACE AT THE TABLE

NOW SEATING IMPOSTER SYNDROME, PARTY OF ... YOU?

By Sheila Buswell

Self-doubt is, at its core, a sense that you are "not enough." In this book, I wanted to show how people have overcome that universal feeling. There are many ways we are made to feel we are not enough. There are just as many ways to move past such sentiments. To help the reader accomplish this, this chapter will offer some personal solutions, as well as some cultural ones.

When I started building my company, I felt like I didn't know nearly enough about business or computer engineering. I knew I needed to contribute in a meaningful way to that conversation, but I never doubted I could. Society has impressed upon me a need to be able to back up what I say, and it's impossible to definitively say that this need isn't influenced by self-doubt. What I do know is that I never wanted to be one of those people who spoke up when they didn't have any idea what they were talking about. So it was important to gain the knowledge and confidence to speak up intelligently.

People often must pretend to be someone other than who they naturally are. For example, I am not very feminine, but people have certain expectations of me immediately upon meeting me. Just this week, I met someone who assumed I would be scared of math, enjoy shopping, know about child rearing, and have children—and it's not the first time I've encountered such assumptions. This happens in other minority groups as well; people must work hard to live up to expectations, even when that means stepping away from their authentic selves. There are some people who straighten their hair. Some people do not put their names on their resumes—they use initials instead, so businesses won't make negative assumptions. This type of camouflage shouldn't be necessary in 2023.

In my experience, women and minorities are often told they need to look and act a certain way to access certain spaces or positions. So once they achieve placement in management or spaces of power, it makes sense that they would feel like imposters. No one has ever told them they belong, and they've never been allowed to feel they can act naturally. With those internalized messages, it is incredibly difficult not to feel like a fraud.

When one cannot be genuine and "act natural," how can they bring their authentic selves to the workplace? If people can't bring their whole selves into professional spaces, how do they not feel like "imposters?"

When someone works in a field where they are the only person that looks or acts like they do, they must continuously hide their true selves. I have felt this way, and others I have spoken to have as well. And that is a recipe for imposter syndrome. It's difficult enough just to perform well in the workplace—but some face extra challenges on top of that. They may experience the pressures of feeling like they represent their entire race or sex, like they are responsible for the image of their entire culture—and that is obviously an unfair weight for them to carry. This alone could easily cause symptoms associated with imposter syndrome: anxiety, depression, and burnout.

This is something I have experienced personally. I was enlisted in the Army and attached to a Tanker Battalion. After leaving the Army, I found myself the only woman veteran at the place I worked, and I was asked to speak on behalf of all women in the Army. The places I worked after that expected me to "fit" an outdated mold of what an engineer "looks like." This is obviously ridiculous. People are people. We are all different, and neatly categorizing us is impossible. We are not a monolith. I can represent myself, my needs, and my perspective. But I am the only person I can speak about with full understanding. Asking me to be a representative of every female soldier was a fool's errand created by assumptions and prejudice.

It's important that we stop making assumptions and forcing people into boxes just to suit expectations. To solve the problems we face as a society, we need diverse thinking, and diverse people. We will not get diverse thinking if we keep the cultural status quo.

This brings up a part of this discussion about imposter syndrome that is important for everyone to notice. Most people who exhibit behaviors consistent with imposter syndrome are minorities. The fact that this is such a visible demographic tells us that the culture needs to change, not the people. This isn't just one person's insecurities; it's a full campaign to undermine a whole group of people. Self-doubt is real, but it's made so much worse when others encourage people to "fake it till they make it" to get through the situation. If we are not sure about who we are or what we are doing, it should be safe to admit that. All this advice does is pull the doubt and uncertainty deeper down so it's harder to get past.

I am not an expert in sociology, but I believe that a good start to changing culture is to change how we define professionalism. It needs to stop being about "looks." We should set criteria for work accomplishments. In the Army, it didn't matter what the generator mechanic looked like—what mattered was if they were capable of getting the lights on. I feel this would be a good model to follow: a true meritocracy. Reward good work, and let people's characters dictate how they are perceived at their jobs. This strategy would raise up excellent people and rid workplaces of toxic people with poor work ethic who somehow have maintained privilege and protection in the current system. Connect culture and accountability—it's the only way society can move forward.

PART 1

CULTURAL SOLUTIONS

"Leadership is absolutely about inspiring action, but it is also about guarding against mis-action."

—*Simon Sinek*

ules can be good or bad, depending on how they are applied. Unfortunately, rules are often used to reinforce outdated ideas or enforce a dominant culture, and as such, they can be at the root of many doubts and misconceptions. While rules can be used to control people, they should actually be used to create an inclusive environment where good ideas reign supreme. Rules should help ensure that people feel comfortable bringing our best, most authentic selves to work; they should not be used to enforce an idea of what a role "looks" like. In my opinion, imposter syndrome is often created when company culture focuses too much on the "look" of the person performing the task, rather than simply focusing on the task itself.

Rules are used to enforce a company's culture. For years, this meant keeping outdated stereotypes in power, and maintaining a work environment that often excluded people. I believe that is why certain fields have been slow to change. The demographic of the people in positions of power has not really shifted over the past 50 years. While many of those people deserved to be there, some were only there because they looked the part. I also know some awesomely smart people who didn't "look the part" and so were disregarded, even though they should have been the ones leading the way. This is frustrating. It's also demotivating and stifles innovation. If you have tired old stereotypes running things and judging who can and can't contribute, how are you going to get fresh ideas?

Rules should govern skills and behavior, not personality. If one works better in a T-shirt, that is what they should wear. I am an engineer. Salespeople may be more effective in a different suit. I have found that many "dress codes" were silly and even recently didn't include women's attire. Unisex seems to not fit anybody. The unisex shirt I was given had huge sleeves, so I had to wear a shirt underneath or show off my bra, and it couldn't be "tucked in" on me.

I will never be able to wear the same clothes as a man. There are people that wouldn't choose to dress like me. Dress codes should be written for a job function, not perception. When I was working as a generator mechanic, I had coveralls. I feel like dress codes add to imposter syndrome. If dressing is a part of who we are as individuals, how do we bring our authentic selves to work? I do not mean wearing grossly inappropriate things like your Def Leppard or Taylor Swift concert shirt with the sleeves torn off. What I mean is simply asking yourself if this will help me do my job? I like sweatpants, but I look like a hot mess in them and will not even wear them even on a Zoom call. Dress codes can enforce a culture. Women should not be expected to dress like a man to do a job. When one has to wear a costume to fill the requirements of a dress code or a culture that feels foreign, how do you not feel like an imposter? If you are the only woman or minority in a room or at a table, and you are told you need to dress like the dominant culture, how is that not a breeding ground for imposter syndrome?

I have been both "laid off" (which was not personal and often dictated by the market) and "fired" (which was very personal, and was dictated by my perceived work output and the notion that others could do it better). At the time, each experience felt really personal, but with some distance and perspective, I can now honestly state that I was better after both experiences. It's impossible to know the true reasoning of companies when they let people go—but I do know that there were some smart and talented people laid off, and at the same time, slimy, lying, vacuous holes of human beings were kept. This type of thing is hard not to take personally. As a company leader now, it is unimaginable to think of this as a recipe for success and innovation.

When I was laid off, I moved directly on to making more money; indirectly, it led to a path that would define my future. I hear people describe careers as a ladder, but to me, it was more like a jungle gym. I moved up but not in a straight line.

Improvements to Outcome-Based Roles

I have never had an accurate job description. Job descriptions are generally intentionally vague, and I am certain the ones I have participated in writing are just as vague. I can say I am looking for someone to complete the Mechanical Design of the Prototype of the Upward Mobility. This Role is based on the outcome needed and is not vague. I also am going directly to pick the person I think will be best and not base this on who "looks" like they can do the job.

When I was fired, I was told that I made too many mistakes. I cannot say this is untrue, but I will state this: I learned about the quality control system we had. I wrote a test plan for the Occipital Cervical Thoracic (OCT) spinal system I designed. Without guidance, I sent every bit of what I had to the Quality VP at the time, asking her if what I had was enough. She not only didn't respond to my email, but she also used what I sent her as ammunition in the quality review meeting. That lesson was important; empowered people empower other people. It was not an empowered woman who threw me under the bus for asking a question. I was furious, but that was a valuable lesson in retrospect. I think if you have good ideas, and you are good at your job, you are of value. But not all people are on your side; some women and veterans have been affected by the culture and have tried to use me in the past. This has taught me repeatedly that "people are people." I am good and bad depending on the day, and I act accordingly. Don't assume people will help, but be appreciative when they do.

Align Culture with Strategy

If you have a culture that has outdated ideas and is toxic, then you will have a hard time developing an innovative strategy. This strategy should align with the way the world works in the present. Company cultures should be up to date and focused on including as much diversity as possible so the pool of ideas can grow. People should not only be welcomed to work as their authentic selves, but this should be actively encouraged by rules and outcomes as well. The repercussions of being authentic should never be a source of fear; otherwise, people will feel like imposters. If no one is forced to use brain space trying to be someone they are not, there will be less room for self-doubt and more room for innovation.

Connect Culture and Accountability

Fire bad employees who do not connect with the company culture. In the past, employees were "let go" for a nebulous perception of what professionals "looked like." Good employees move on to different jobs when bad employees are not corrected.

What should be part of the culture:

- Employees who achieve good outcomes, regardless of how people perceive them, should get promoted.
- Employees who achieve poor outcomes and behave poorly should be fired for the sake of the company.

Define the Non-Negotiable

Definitions of the bare minimum and the absolute rules must be clearer. A non-negotiable policy would be different to me than it might be to someone else. Most people would agree on what should be a fireable offense, but this should be laid out clearly, so everyone knows the policies and procedures are set in stone.

These things should be common sense. I have read books on leadership and been in charge of a shop. I know what impact it can have on employees when they see that bad behavior isn't punished and good behavior isn't rewarded. I didn't care anymore about producing good work when people were not punished for acting poorly. It's easier to maintain employee motivation when people are treated according to how they behave and work within a company.

What Does This Have to Do with Imposter Syndrome?

Cultures that reinforce the idea of what people should be and do through a very narrow lens need to stop imposing restrictive rules just to maintain the status quo. These cultures can make some people feel they must behave a certain way to belong, even if that way harms them or reduces their confidence. This is how they create imposters. When these imposters are in positions of power, they may question themselves. However, if the people from the top down make even small changes in the company culture, people may feel more included, confident, and invested. These small changes can make a huge difference.

Bad behavior should not be tolerated. Good ideas should be rewarded and celebrated. This would produce a good culture. It would not eliminate all self-doubt or occurrences of imposter syndrome, but it would level the playing field.

If it is in your power, create an environment where people who have good ideas and have knowledge to impart are welcome at the table, regardless of arbitrary and hard-to-define standards of professionalism. If they have good ideas, welcome and support them. Create a table where seats are earned by ideas. Let this create the culture.

We spend way too much time preparing for and working to allow ourselves to feel like we do not belong there. There are too many problems that need to be solved. We all need to get over our negative feelings and work together to solve the problems that face our society.

PART 2

PERSONAL SOLUTIONS

"We are what we believe we are."

— *C. S. Lewis*

Many people feel like they do not belong. It seems to me that while feeling like a fish out of water can be uncomfortable, it can also motivate someone to reach greater heights.

I have not set out to accomplish great things, but as I showed early on in life, I do not like to be told I can't. I feel that in many ways this feeling motivated me to work harder, learn more, and prove my place. For example, I ran a marathon only because I was told I would not run again. I feel like you can choose to be uncomfortable as a fish out of water, or simply look for higher ground. I was not going to be made to "feel" like I didn't belong at a table with other engineers; I belonged there.

I have come to believe that anyone can experience imposter syndrome, no matter what position they hold, what race they are, or what gender they represent. They can feel it based on being older than their peers, or younger. They can feel it just because they look a certain way—and that can apply to a white male, or a person of color, or both. If they feel different from the other people around them, imposter syndrome can easily take over. Everyone faces the expectations of others and works hard to live up to them, even if there's very little validity behind those expectations. This is why I think it is dangerous to dictate an ideal of what a role "should look" like. The idea that there is a "look" for generator mechanic, veteran, engineer, or CEO is silly. I avoided feeling like I wasn't enough in these circumstances because of my path. In other ways I have a "look" that traditionally has meant to people that I would be maternal, love to hold babies, and know my way around a make-up counter. These ideas are exclusionary and in many ways harmful. I was in the Army for almost four years and yet I will never forget the time I parked in the "parking for Veterans" spot at Lowes and a women yelled out at me, "You don't get to park there because your husband is a Veteran." Why did she make that assumption? Why did she think it was OK to yell that out of a passenger side window as she drove by? Why am I still bothered by it 15 years later?

I do not think we should let the society we live in decide our place. I think most women today would rebel against being told they belonged "in a kitchen." Why then is it assumed that certain people belong in an office? Regardless of what you look like, do what you want. I am not an expert but I think this may be part of why people end up in careers they don't thrive in. If you are not comfortable in your skin I don't think you can bring your best self to work. This is regardless of the package you are wrapped in. If you are not a minority in your field—or even if you are—you should still feel like you belong there based on more than just a "look." My husband has the "look" of an engineer, but he is a great cook. Perhaps the world missed out on his true calling.

For me, my imposter syndrome came from feeling out of place, not because I was a woman in engineering, but because I was a woman in engineering who didn't have the behavior or preferences of the average woman. I worked hard to make sure I knew my stuff so I could avoid having those feelings of inadequacy.

There is so much stress surrounding this need to prove that you belong somewhere. While there's no easy solution, creating a culture that does not judge a book by its cover would be a solid start.

It is not bad that we all suffer from self-doubt, but if we can tap into why we collectively do what we do, we can hopefully provide a solution to the problem.

I stand by the idea that aligning culture with strategy can help make this happen. Making sure company values align with employee support can make people and their opinions feel valued, which is a vital component of removing self-doubt from the workplace.

But there are also personal changes one can make outside of work that can help ease the suffering caused by imposter syndrome. I myself am not by any means a finished product ready to be placed under glass. I do not have all the answers; there are so many ways I feel inadequate. I am a work in progress still dealing with the current cultural norms. But I do want to share some tactics that have worked for me over the years—ways to help remind yourself that you, too, have value.

- Remember Your Past Achievements
- Don't Compare Yourself to Others
- Practice Self-Grace
- Be Mindful of Your Thinking
- Will This Matter in a Year?

Remember Past Achievements

As I write this, I can see that this is a personal solution I employed often. When I left the Army, I would often approach mechanical engineering classes filled with people much younger and more knowledgeable who'd just left a high school that had prepared them for this (I thought). In these situations of potential self-doubt, I would think about my military experience. I had made it through Basic Training, Bosnia, Field Rotations. There were so many past milestones that I had achieved, and remembering them helped me maintain a sense of confidence even in uncomfortable situations.

I would also use this mentality with distance in running races. I would think to myself, if I ran a 5K and won, I can run a 10K. If I can run a 10K, I can run a half marathon, and so on—right up to full marathons, biathlons, and triathlons. Simply adding to what I had done before in small increments.

No matter what I found myself facing, I knew I could do it—I just had to dig a little deeper.

Basic Training taught me a lot. Many of the sayings like "Winners find reasons, losers find excuses" would flash through my mind in moments like this. As I get older, I realize I accomplished a lot in my early years. I use these accomplishments to fuel other accomplishments. I convinced myself that I could do whatever it was if I had a reason. I ran races most weekends when I could.

In 2018, my older sister died. It was sad—but more than that, I had to be restrained in my actions, and examine them. There are times when not being able to do anything is just brutal. Helping plan her funeral and ease the suffering of others was the hardest thing I have ever had to do. Now I use that as the new metric. Whatever I'm facing, it may be hard, but not nearly as hard as my sister's death, and I lived through that, so…

There were times when "Remembering Past Achievements" didn't work. Working through engineering school took bravery and constant reminding that I belonged there. I still had to do my homework and strived hard to understand concepts. And when it came to running, I constantly had to increase the lengths of my training runs—I couldn't just depend on knowing I had once done something. I remember once taking a Pilates class on a cruise we were all on for my parents' 50th wedding anniversary. I was simply sick of running around a ship trying to get distance, and so I took the class, thinking I was at least cross-training. It was a 90-minute class, and though I was running a lot, I lacked any core strength. I remember being cocky, thinking, "Well I can do this—it will be easy." But it was so, so hard. I remember I even said out loud (and am often quoted as such at family events), "Is it supposed to hurt this much?"

I had a run a marathon at this time, and I could do a great deal of pushups. But Pilates was so different, requiring a strength and flexibility that frankly I had never trained for. I was an imposter in that Pilates class—it isn't just that I felt like one. I think the distinction between feeling like an imposter and being an imposter is decided by you. Do you belong there?

During the pandemic I was diagnosed with a degenerative nerve disorder called Hereditary Spastic Paraparesis. This is a disease that slowly reduces your ability to build muscle in certain areas. I can't run anymore. I can barely walk. I need to be mentally tough every day as my identity is challenged. I need to be tough mentally when people think I am drunk at the grocery store as I wobble. I need be mentally tough when people assume I am older than I am as I move like I am

112 years old. I need to focus on what I can do, not what I used to do. I started weight training. After that Pilates class, I never made the mistake again of assuming things would be easy. Mentally, I am stronger from that Pilates class—as I learned that although it is good to remember your past achievements, just because you did one hard thing this doesn't mean you can do all hard things without training and preparation. Make an assumption like that and you will wind up humbled and often quoted.

I am certain Mike Tyson is strong, and so is Boris Becker, but they are a different kind of strong. Both boxing and tennis take training and practice, and neither is inherently better than the other—they're just different. Mike Tyson and Boris Becker were both top in their sports, and they know you don't just get there by showing up one day.

I think it is a good tool to remember your past achievements, but I also think it is important to appreciate that practice and training is needed to accomplish tasks. And it's OK to be a beginner—this is where self-grace comes in. I have no doubt that I could have been proficient at Pilates (or make up, hair, and babies) but I didn't practice and I didn't train. Imposter syndrome is many things to many people, but to me, if you prepare, you belong there. Even with preparation, your brain may make you feel like an imposter, but if you actually have not prepared, then you really are just faking it and are an imposter after all.

In Ingrid's story, she doesn't initially give herself enough credit for all the degrees she earned and the hard work she put in. Even though she took a really difficult path, her mind played tricks on her, convincing her that she didn't belong where she was. It wasn't until others pointed out to her how special she was that she allowed herself to realize she'd always been enough.

In Mary's story, she comes to a new country, gets an advanced degree, learns a new language, obtains two patents, and authors multiple publications, yet still manages to doubt her self-worth. There is no easy pill to make imposter syndrome go away, but I wonder if taking inventory of her many accomplishments could have helped Mary when she found herself in need.

Stacey does a great job of remembering past achievements when she goes for her interview and gets the job, but as the job progresses, she loses sight of how lucky they were to have her, and her thinking and habits go negative. Fortunately, Stacey reorients herself away from self-doubt and returns to a place of positivity. She puts boundaries in place and learns to treat herself with patience and kindness.

Don't Compare Yourself to Others

In the past, before social media, I often used to compare myself to others. I found it motivating: if this person could do something, then I could, also. Social media has changed this in my view—now, people compare themselves to a highlight reel, and that is simply not fair.

For years I practiced yoga, which has been beneficial to me for many reasons. Besides being able to touch my toes now, I also learned to simply "stay on my mat." I am very competitive by nature. When I was in the military, I was going to be the best in physical training or PT in my shop, which was mostly male. Simply meeting the physical standards wasn't enough. I worked out multiple times a day to ensure that I could do what the male solders were required to do to obtain a 300 on their Army Physical Fitness Test (APFT). For me, it was not simply about having goals and achieving them, it was about not allowing people to pass me. Although I am not an expert, I feel pretty certain this was because I was insecure and needed validation. I was this way in school as well—I always needed to get the best score in the class. There was a great deal of good in this mindset, and it did pay dividends, but I am no longer that person now. I do not really compete or compare myself with others, and I am far happier as a result.

When I ran my first marathon, I was motivated by knowing someone who had run marathons as well. If he could do it, I knew I could do it—after all, I was mentally tougher and grittier. In turn, I knew a woman who was smarter and tougher than me—Kate Mansker, one of the contributors to this book. I made her my running buddy and although we lived far apart, we kept in touch and did a few long runs together. She ran the first marathon with me—well, she beat me by an hour, so we didn't actually run together. In a way it was great that I ran a marathon, but in my mind the fact that she not only ran the marathon but dominated the course made me so proud. I found joy in her success and her many successes since then (she has found a love of triathlons, too, and she even holds a Guinness World Record for long distance paddling.) I find her inspirational, and am not jealous at all. I have no desire to compete with her, and I always look forward to seeing what Kate Mansker does next.

Comparing yourself to others is just so easy. We do it all the time without even thinking about it. But when you notice yourself doing it, keep in mind that you don't know all the things that the other person is going through. Besides, when it comes to your own journey, does anyone else's honestly even matter?

In his journey to become a nurse, Peter compared himself to his peers. It is so hard not to do this, as it is our nature to constantly assess how we fit in a room. It was only after he was around patients and working as an educator that he began to feel confident in his abilities, like he really belonged where he was. There were so many times I was the "only woman," but instead of comparing myself to those around me and noticing the differences, I focused on our similarities—after all, I was not just a woman in a room full of men, I was an engineer in a room full of engineers: I belonged there.

My brother went to Malawi, Africa to teach after 9/11. He told me a story of a woman who walked two miles to the hospital to give birth, and then walked home the next day with her husband and new born baby. I live in America—there is no way I would even consider this. Hard is different for different people and easy is different for different people. I had a full-on meltdown over mascara on Tuesday, although there are people that would think choosing mascara is easy. I think changing a tire is easy. What's hard for some is easy for others—it's all personal, in the end. There comes a point when comparisons lose all meaning.

It would have been easy for Betsey to compare herself to those around her—after all, unlike so many in the room, she wasn't even a veteran—but she found a way to move beyond such comparisons and discover her own innate value. What she brought to the table—herself—was, in the end, incomparable. Objective Zero is a great app, and I am sure a lot of people are still around because of Betsey and her perseverance.

Practice Self-Grace

I have to admit: I struggle with this. When I look back, this idea seems at odds with the notion of "finding reasons not excuses." When I talk about self-grace, I don't mean to encourage behaviors that are substandard. I mean instead that we should not beat ourselves up over things that cannot be changed. For instance, I probably will not play for the WNBA. Besides the obvious height disparity, I lack hand-eye coordination, I have not practiced, and honestly, I'm not even a fan. Looking back, I shouldn't have beaten myself up over Pilates being hard. I should have either worked to better myself at it or accepted that it was something that takes a level of training that I had not done.

To me, self-grace is about accepting where I am and taking inventory of what it would take to get where I want to go. Problems don't get solved and stuff doesn't get done by simply beating oneself up over something that can't be changed. There are so many things that we are not, but there is little point in focusing on this. Instead, we need to appreciate who we are and focus on what we can do. Sure, I will never play pro basketball, but Michael Jordan or LeBron James will probably not invent something that can reduce lawsuits in rehabilitation hospitals.

Stacey does a great job of accepting that she had been pushing herself too hard. She adjusts, setting boundaries around her mental health and making that a priority. She sets a solid lunch time where she refuses to be interrupted. She lets one incident get to her, but then she recovers and comes back stronger.

After years of battling herself and not feeling good enough, Ingrid finally accepts herself for who she is. She recognizes that she is enough, and that she holds tremendous value just as she is. The fact she begins to be appreciated by others also helps her accept her self-worth.

The other contributors also arrived at a sense of self-acceptance. Betsey figured out that she didn't need to be a veteran to be of value in her work at the non-profit: She recognized that she added immense value just being herself. And in his story, once Peter began to be more open with those around him about the fact he was not an experienced nurse, this allowed him a certain grace—he could be himself without having to worry about pretending to be anyone else, and this was an enormous relief.

Roseline faced numerous challenges that made her doubt her self-worth. But when she comes to understand that her story is worth telling, and that it could help others out there in need, this allows her to practice self-grace, accept her fears of failure, and move onward and upward. It can be hard to allow self-grace into our lives, but it is important to do as it frees us up to get the help we need to continue.

Be Mindful of Your Thinking

Sometimes when I catch myself, I am generally already well on my way down a path of negative self-talk. I am not a huge Henry Ford fan, but I believe he was right when he said, "Whether you think you can, or you think you can't—you're right." It does no good to dwell on the failed relationships and mistakes in your life. Such negative thinking can alter your future: after all, if you're convinced you will fail, you probably will.

Instead, convince yourself that you can! Like John Burroughs said, "If you think you can do it, you can."

I feel this is almost the flip side to "Remembering Your Past Achievements." Don't linger on what your failures were—use them to adjust and avoid similar missteps. Learn from mistakes, but don't wallow in them.

Ingrid's story illuminates how her negative thinking kept her from really being able to inventory her past achievements. Her mind kept repeating to her that others deserved to be here or there but that she did not, and she believed these thoughts, even though they had no real basis in reality. Ingrid is brilliant and strong, and she definitely deserves to be in those places—the Army is so lucky to have her.

Imposter syndrome can trap us in negative thought patterns, and in Ingrid's case, one of the things that helped her escape her negative self-talk and made her see her self-worth was the fact that others expressed their gratitude to her. Perhaps we need to call on friends and family to remind us that we are enough in these situations.

Peter focused on what set him apart instead of on how wonderful and well-prepared he was. His thinking was also negative and didn't help the situation. Too often, we are inclined to let our imposter syndrome do the talking in our heads. If we remind ourselves that these thoughts are just thoughts, and that they do not necessarily have any basis in reality, then they do not have to control us. We can be free from them and take positive action: in Peter's case, this meant doing what he could to help and contribute, and the result was that patients and students benefited from his expertise.

Instead of focusing on what she did know, Kate focused on what she didn't know in the "freshman phase" of her career. Later in her career, she does a great job of refocusing her thinking. In so many ways, the "freshman phase" terminology is appropriate. In this stage of our careers, we let that feeling of not being enough take the "wheel," but as we become more confident and progress into our sophomore, junior, and senior years, the imposter feeling takes a back seat, even if it never really goes away completely. Me, I am a senior in engineering, but a freshman in many other areas of life—and that's OK. There's no need for me to let my thinking about women and babies spiral out of control—instead, I need to recognize that these are just thoughts. I need to practice self-grace, accept where I am, and move forward from here to solve this problem.

Rosaline doesn't allow the events in her life to define her. She digs within herself to define herself on her own terms. That being said, in the end Roseline thinks about the negative implications of her book instead of its true intent: to help people. Her thinking eventually got back on track, but it is important to be mindful, as our thinking can derail us. I am often well down the negative spiral before I catch myself. This is a practice that gets easier to employ once the pattern has been identified.

Will This Matter in a Year?

Through my life there have been moments that mattered and many that just didn't. I have sat at many tables that were hostile at first. People didn't want me there, and I was often challenged about how I knew things or why I said this or that. This is an area where I chose my battles, like many situations in life. I often questioned the lasting impact of an event as a simple way to determine if a battle was worth fighting. (Sadly, I didn't always choose correctly, but I did my best). Sometimes, I knowingly endured mistreatment, even though I knew it was wrong, because I was aware I was gaining lasting knowledge, and the fact that I was being treated poorly was only temporary. Other times, I knew I needed to say something to shut down a conversation, because it was on its way to having a lasting negative impact. I was not always very articulate at these moments—I think once I even yelled, "Kittens are furry!" to change the subject.

Roseline does a great job of navigating what will matter in the long term and what will not. She reports a rape. Later, she allows one incident of inappropriateness to pass, but issues a complaint when it happens over and over. Even though she is still plagued by imposter syndrome, her ability to judge what matters and what doesn't helps her overcome it in the end.

Betsey had the experience and the education needed to head that non-profit. The arbitrary qualities people initially judged her by didn't matter in the long term. Betsey knew that the work she was doing mattered far more than what people thought of her, so she stuck with it. She had her priorities in line. She knew what she knew and didn't pretend she wasn't what she wasn't. I think there is power in that kind of wisdom and humility.

Between myself and all the other contributors, I feel we combined these personal solutions to navigate a life filled with self-doubt and achieve success. None of us are by any means done, and I am certain that we will continue to fight battles.

Personally, I have practiced these ideas and found they helped me when I didn't get the respect I felt I deserved. When I felt imposter syndrome creeping in around the edges, these solutions helped me restore belief in myself, and in my innate worth. I have sat at tables where initially I was not welcomed, and my input was not desired, but I knew nevertheless that I belonged there. I didn't ask for a seat—I just sat down.

NOTES ON CONTRIBUTORS

Stacey Brown, MBA is a US Army veteran. After earning a bachelor's degree in communications in 2005, she would soon enter management training in one of the largest private companies in the U.S. It was there that she developed a love for travel. Several promotions, and three regional moves later, Stacey decided to seek a career change. She enlisted in the Army Corps of Engineers in 2012 and deployed to Bagram, Afghanistan in support of Operation Enduring Freedom. After completing that overseas opportunity, she was then reassigned to Baltimore, Maryland where she graduated from Defense Information School (DINFOS) in 2016. Immediately upon completing reclassification school, she was tasked with spending her final deployment as a Public Affairs Coordinator at Naval Station Guantanamo Bay. Upon military separation and reentrance into the civilian sector, Stacey enrolled in an MBA program with a concentration in Project Management. She formed Military Travel, LLC during the height of the pandemic. Since graduating in the Summer of 2022, she now focuses on her business where she uses past experiences as a travel administrator to leverage procurement opportunities for other service-disabled veteran owned small businesses (SDVOSB). Stacey is pursuing her business, Military Travel, LLC in metropolitan Atlanta, GA.

Please also find Stacey on LinkedIn.

Sheila Buswell is the CEO/ Co-Founder of Buswell Biomedical. She developed the concept for the Upward Mobility in 2018 and started Buswell Biomedical with her husband, Gregg, in 2019. In 1997, she joined the Army, injuring her foot in Bosnia in 1998. After receiving a medical discharge in 2001, Sheila moved to Missouri to continue her education and help her sister with babysitting. She earned a BS in Mechanical Engineering in 2005 from Missouri University of Science and Technology (then UMR). Sheila holds an MS in Biomedical Engineering from Saint Louis University.

Sheila ran two marathons and more sprint triathlons than she can remember—and when she could not run, she did yoga. She was diagnosed with Hereditary Spastic Paraparesis in 2020 and started weight training. She loves to camp, and has traveled the country with her husband, Gregg and her dog, Penne.

Please also find Sheila on LinkedIn.

Mary Imani: After coming to the United States, Mary started a master's degree in chemistry at Southern Illinois University of Edwardsville in 2012. When she graduated a year later, she was accepted into the PhD program of the University of Missouri-Columbia. Mary worked for almost four years for Eurofins before joining the pharma group of the company that she is working for now.

Mary now works in the research and development department, and is part of the team that focuses on developing monoclonal antibodies used to treat a wide range of diseases, including cancers, autoimmune, hereditary, and more.

Kate (Pfefferkorn) Mansker graduated from the University of Missouri-Columbia with a degree in Chemical Engineering. She owns Pfefferkorn Engineering & Environmental. Kate is married to Scott. She has a son, a stepdaughter, and a stepson.

After running her first marathon at age 21, Kate spent her free time training for and participating in triathlons, marathons and ultramarathon paddling races. Kate was also in the 2012 Guinness Book of World Records for having paddled the furthest distance in twenty-four hours on moving water by a female.

While in college, Kate started the student chapter of Engineers Without Borders at the University of Missouri-Columbia. During this time, she participated in a geotechnical stabilization project in a rural Bolivian village in the Andes Mountains.

Betsey Mercado earned a BA in Business Administration from the American Public University System and holds a MS in Human Services from Purdue University. Deeply committed to serving Army families and the military community, she has over 20 years of experience volunteering with a variety of Army and military units and various nonprofits.

Betsey is a co-founder and Executive Director of the Objective Zero Foundation, a tech nonprofit focused on the social connectedness and wellness of service members, veterans, their families, and caregivers. In this capacity Betsey has trained more than 2,500 suicide prevention peer support volunteers and served more than 14,000 service-members using mobile-app technology to provide peer support, training, and access to health and wellness resources.

Betsey is on the Military Officers Association of America's Currently Serving Spouse Advisory Board, where she informs MOAA about issues that impact military families. She is also a member of the Evacuate Our Allies Coalition, the Sioux Falls Veteran Suicide Prevention Coalition, Bunker Labs 21 B & 22A Cohorts, and has the distinction of partnering with the Centers for Disease Control and Prevention and CDC Foundation's Veteran Suicide Prevention Evaluation Project.

Betsey is a recipient of the Shield of Sparta - Heroine of the Infantry Award, a finalist for Fast Company's World Changing Ideas Award, and the Commander's Award for Public Service. Her mobile app, the Objective Zero App, was a finalist for the Congressional Medal of Honor Society's Citizen Honors Award, a FourSquare for Good recipient, a Gold Edison Award, and was the 'Best New Mobile App' of 2019. The Objective Zero Foundation received the Newman's Own Award and the CTIA Wireless Foundation's Catalyst Award.

Roseline Salazar was born and raised in Honolulu, Hawaii and currently resides in Columbus, Ohio. She is a retired Air Force Veteran and a #1 Best Selling International Published Author with a passion to help veterans discover their purpose after the military. She is the author of *Make a Smooth Transition after the Military: Create Yourself a Wonderful Civilian Life* and the co-author of *PTSD Compass: How to Recover from PTSD and Navigate Trauma to Triumph.*

After almost six years as an enlisted Airman, Roseline earned her commission through the US Air Force Reserve Officer Training Corps (ROTC) at the University of Hawaii Detachment 175. She holds an M.S. in management with a concentration in human resources from Troy University, a B.S. in information systems management from the University of Maryland University College, an A.S. in Paralegal Studies from the Kapiolani Community College, and an A.S. in Transportation from the Community College of the Air Force. Roseline was an enlisted Traffic Management Journeyman prior to becoming a Communications and Logistics Officer. She was also deployed to Prince Sultan Air Base in Saudi Arabia, Balad Air Base in Iraq, and Camp Clark in Khowst, Afghanistan.

Roseline is a board-certified mental health coach. As she continues her journey as a published author, she looks forward to helping with the issues our military communities are facing.

Peter D. Smith, BA, MSN, RN, CNE, is an educator at Lindenwood University in the College of Science, Technology, and Health. He earned his BSN in 2010 and immediately began practicing as a critical care nurse. He also began educating as a clinical instructor and floor preceptor. He completed his MSN in 2014 and will earn his EdD in 2025. Throughout his career, he has been immersed in patient care activities, client advocacies, and evidence-based practices to advance the art and discipline of nursing.

Joining Lindenwood University in November of 2021, Instructor Peter Smith brought with him a background rich in content that sustains the nursing discipline's platform: Fundamentals, Foundations, Health Assessment, Adult Health, Pathophysiology, Pharmacology, Simulation, and NCLEX preparatory strategies. Dedicated to creating an exceptional learning experience, critical thinking is the underpinning upon which he conducts his didactic, laboratory, simulated, and clinical activities. Instructor Smith earned his BSN in 2010 and immediately began practicing as a critical care nurse and educating as a clinical instructor and floor preceptor. Soon after, he entered an MSN program with a nurse-educator focus, which he completed in 2014. Since then, he has been immersed in patient care activities, client advocacies, and evidence-based practices that have resulted in safe and effective patient care. His hospital experience includes Med-Surg, ENT/Plastics Reconstructive, Trauma, Cardio-Thoracic, and Critical and Progressive Care. To these ends, he has been educating and nursing for several years and has been fortunate enough to work for renowned hospitals and institutions of higher education. Education is one of his passions, and he is currently enrolled in a doctoral program, which will result in his earning his EdD in 2026. In addition, he practices as a Subject Matter Expert by consulting on nursing content, revising NCLEX strategies and questions, and reviewing/editing pre-published nursing textbooks. He also possesses a BA in Communications and retains licensure as an RN in the state of Missouri (a compact state) and is certified as a BLS and ACLS provider, as well as a previous BLS instructor.

Ingrid Weissenfuh is the Director/Founder of the intuitive Safety Group, Inc. She is a graduate (CSP) from the Board of Certified Safety Professionals. Her practical application and scaled measures to enhance sustainable safety turned into a formal business in November of 2021. She joined the Army as an Ordnance officer in 2008. A native of Pascagoula, Mississippi, she currently works as the safety director for an organization with over 33,000 members.

During the spring of 2008, Ingrid attended the DCC (Direct Commission Course) and BOLC II (Basic Officer Leadership Course Phase II) at Fort Benning, GA. She became a qualified Ordnance Officer after attending Army Logistics University at Fort Lee, VA in 2008. In October 2015, Ingrid completed the Multi-Functional Logistics Captain's Career Course. In November 2020, Ingrid completed her AOC and holds the functional area of FA 30 Information Operations. Ingrid has been deployed to Haiti in support of Operation Unified Response in 2010, where she served as Headquarters Element Safety Officer, Unit Movement Officer for Golf Del Mas site, and contract management cell manager. Ingrid has also deployed to Afghanistan in support of Operation Enduring Freedom, 2012. During the aforementioned Afghanistan deployment, she served as a Detainee Officer of The Joint Legal Center at the Detention Facility in Parwan as well as the Joint Legal Center Training Officer. In 2018 she deployed as the OIC of the 54th Military History Detachment to Kuwait, Iraq, and Syria. Her additional deployments include Honduras, Dominican Republic, and Cuba in support of detainee operations and humanitarian support.

Printed in Great Britain
by Amazon

34309573R00076